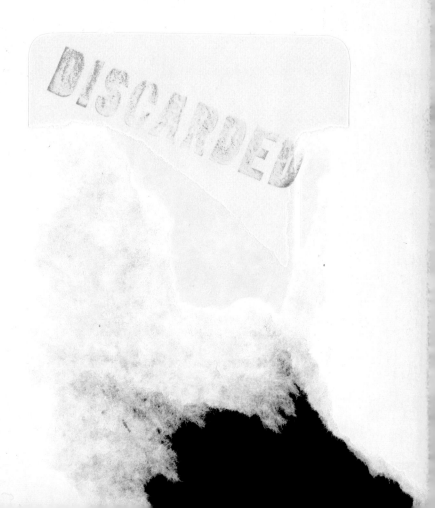

I'VE BEEN AROUND

and around

and around

and around . . .

Illustrations are by Leo Rampen

GEORGE BAIN

I've Been Around

and around
and around
and around...

CLARKE, IRWIN & COMPANY LIMITED
TORONTO   1964   VANCOUVER

Contents

Introduction

In the late 1930's, when the earth's crust had not yet cooled and everything was a lot simpler, Hollywood made a number of movies which portrayed newspaper correspondents as dashing fellows. They were always down on one knee saying to some dying man, "Don't try to talk now, Kurt; have you the plans for the new bomber?", or catching the last train from Prague, or being chased at ninety miles an hour down a dusty road by grey-uniformed men in an open Mercedes-Benz.

Obviously a good life and a full one. These correspondents, inevitably, were tall, lean-jawed men with eyes like hawks, dressed in rakish felt hats and belted trenchcoats. When not otherwise employed, they spent a lot of time with one foot up against the bedroom door fending off some ravening contessa.

They had all been to Shanghai in the good old days and asked one another cryptic questions about Natasha and Serge (pronounced "Ser-gay"). If they drank a lot, they were never the worse for it. They had never heard of the perils of smoking cigarettes, and would not have cared if they had, because cigarettes and coffee were what a man lived on. If they went to bed at all, it only meant that they had lost the unequal struggle with the contessa. *C'est la guerre.*

Nevertheless, their souls remained unstained through it all, and they remained true, in spirit at least, to that little gal in the city room back home who wrote the exposés about the crooked politicians and talked to the City Editor out of the corner of her mouth. She was invariably Glenda Farrell.

This book is composed of a number of pieces which have nothing to do with carryings on like that. But, on with the narrative.

It was about then that I bought a trenchcoat with shoulder straps, an extra flap of material across the shoulders to keep out the Continental rains, and brass eyelets in the belt, and resolved that the first time a contessa tried to break down *my* door, she'd find that I could be as good a loser as the next man. It must have been about that time as well that there began to be a sharp decline in the ravening contessa business—but that was a deduction made only years later.

By then it was much too late. It probably would not have made much difference if I *had* known that I would be spared the importunings of some love-distracted charmer. Once a man is launched in the newspaper business and caught up in the giddying whirl of Toronto City Council, it is hard to pull out and make a fresh start as a pipe fitter's apprentice, especially in a belted trenchcoat.

From Toronto City Council, of course, it is but a step to the even giddier world of Queen's Park, where the Provincial government resides, and from there but another step to the gay, cosmopolitan milieu of Ottawa, the Paris of the Quebec-Ontario border (at least between Arnprior and Montebello).

So five years were spent in Ottawa, glorying in the soaring flights and incandescent brilliance of parliamentary debate and marvelling at the perceptions of great men. Certainly there's nothing in this book about anything like *that*. But on with the narrative.

Now, Ottawa unquestionably is the finest national capital we have (assuming that by publication date it has not been moved to Trois Rivières), but, an inner voice kept crying, "Is this all?" (It is dogma in the Parliamentary Press Gallery that Ottawa *is* all, and ever more shall be-o.) And there were other inducements.

It is one of the little distinctions observed by *The Globe and Mail,* the newspaper for which most of the pieces that follow were committed, that the man employed on home soil is identified as a *reporter,* whereas the one employed abroad is elevated (if that is the word) to the rank of *correspondent.*

The latter title is largely honorific, but some perquisites *do* attach to it. The bearer, for instance, is entitled to be paid in the foreign currency of his choice; the first two items of any expense account are not subject to review by the accounting department so long as they do not (together) amount to more than $7.50; and spurs may be worn in the newsroom while on home leave.

Dangle rewards like that in front of a graduate of the Warner Bros. School of Journalism, and especially one who has kept his trenchcoat regularly drenched with moth spray in his closet for twenty years, and you have someone who is panting for service abroad.

At this juncture, it is necessary to say something about the changes that have overtaken the corresponding business since World War II. The belted trenchcoat is *Out* (the moths might as well have had it after all), so are cigarettes, immoderate drinking, Shanghai, and trains from Prague (or anywhere else). The last ravening contessa was taken as a prize of war in 1942 and is now to be found, stuffed, in the British Museum.

Those things which are *In* include blue Oxford cloth shirts with button-down collars; horn-rimmed glasses; Dubonnet on the rocks; sitting up all night in airplanes; and a passionate interest in international liquidity arrangements, the linear approach to tariff reduction, and contingent provisions for Basle credits from European central banks on the 1961 model.

Nothing, not one scrap, that is to be found in the following pages has anything to do with anything like *that*.

Neither is there anything here about the two Summit conferences and a packet of lesser conferences, United States-British intervention in the Middle East in 1958, the war in Algeria, the coming to power of General de Gaulle, the perpetual worries over whither is the North Atlantic Treaty Organization drifting, Britain's bid to join the Common Market, independent nuclear deterrents, race troubles in the Southern States, the great Cuban missile crisis, the Alaska earthquake, and various elections in Canada, Britain and the United States—except perhaps by oblique and unavoidable reference.

This, as any reasonable person would agree, has taken some doing, since all of these are matters with which correspondents, including this one, have had to deal in the past few years. It is safe, and perhaps will not be considered immodest to say, that, whatever the great issue of the past decade anyone may care to name, it will not be found to have been dealt with in this book in any substantial way.

It gives one an eerie feeling to think of it—or it does me.

UNDERSTANDING

How to avoid it — nations-wise

And the Royal's foreclosed
on the puh-lace out the back

In the Soviet Union, every living-place—state-owned, of course—is bugged with microphones from which lines run to the vast headquarters of SMERSH in the cellars under the Lubianka prison. An incautious word from the man of the house, whispered across the table to his wife (unfortunately, the centrepiece contains a microphone hidden in the stamen of a cornflower), and the next day finds him tailed by an agent with his hat pulled down over dark glasses and his raincoat collar turned up. Soon the householder disappears, never to be heard from again.

These things are well known. It is curious in the circumstances how little is known the other way around; how many misconceptions about our way of life continue to flourish in the Soviet Union. It's curious, that is, until one takes a hinge at some of the ideas about Canada propagated in the six pages devoted to that subject in the *New Soviet Encyclopædia.*

To gauge their effect, we look in upon two sturdy peasant types, knitting their brows as they pore over a thick volume on the table in front of them. They are Stefan Lombardnik, whose scholarship and industry have made him the pride of Collective Farm Eight, and his younger brother, Guy, who is known as the sweetest *mouzhik* this side of Stefan.

The volume: Volume 19 of the *Large Soviet Encyclopædia.* The section: Canada. The subject: Agriculture. Stefan reads: "Agriculture is, in fact, dominated by the banks. They seize farms under the guise of assistance, via one-sided loans, and then they expropriate the land and all the property of the farmers."

A tear stains the page as Stefan meditates on the plight of the Canadian farmer. And as he and his brother sit in silent communion with the oppressed of the prairies, a vision of that wretched life unfolds before them:

3

[We are in a Saskatchewan farmhouse. From a window we can see the fields of waving wheat and in the distance an oil derrick. The view is only partly obscured by the corner of the two-car garage. And in the house two people confront one another: golden-haired Prudence Pennyweight, that year's Miss Wheat Belt, and a man whose tall silk hat and black cape proclaim him a banker.]

BANKER: You will marry me, mah proud beauty, or I shall foreclose the mortgage on the oil-well, thereby depriving your parents, Prodigal J. Pennyweight, and his devoted wife, Emma, of the wherewithal to flee next winter's icy blasts to the balmy breezes of Tampa.

PRUDENCE: But, Sir, I cannot marry you, because I am already betrothed to Horace Trueblood, him that is known far and wide as the very embodiment of all that is honourable and manly.

[From outside there come sounds of a horse galloping and in a moment Horace Trueblood, for indeed it is none other, bursts in and hurls himself between Prudence and her unwelcome suitor.]

TRUEBLOOD: Here you villain, is sufficient to satisfy your mean claim against the parents of this fair girl, to whom it is plain for all to see that my heart has been lost. Leave, and if you should so much as speak to this maid again, I promise that I shall thrash you within an inch of your miserable life!

BANKER: Curses! Foiled again!

[Fiercely stroking the ends of his moustache, the banker, Cyril Sidewinder (hiss, hiss), the wealthiest and meanest man (hiss, hiss) in all Unity, Saskatchewan (hiss, hiss), slinks out. As he goes Prudence and Horace are joined by the elder Pennyweights. Joining hands, they sing the Canadian farm song, knowing full well that it is only for the moment that they have been saved.]

> "Montreal, My Bank"—what cynical prattle,
> Their man has just been, and gone off with the cattle,
> From chassis to motor, to last gear and pinion
> Our thresher's been seized by Toronto-Dominion;
> These acres of legumes, of tubers and cereals,
> We fear are not ours but, instead, are Imperial's.
> Now Barclay's is seizing the house, and, alack,
> The Royal's foreclosed on the place out the back.

As the vision fades before the eyes of the Lombardniks in far-off Russia, there can be heard in the background repeated softly and with feeling, *And the Royal's fore-closed on the puh-lace (we mean the puh-lace) out thuh back.*

With streaming eyes, Stefan and his brother turn once more to their reading of the Canadian section. Under the heading, "Education," they read: "The curricula and methods of teaching in Canadian schools are ruled by American pedagogy. Science is replaced by the propaganda of racism, chauvinism and militarism."

Once more the print fades and there rises before them a scene of a typical Canadian schoolroom, Grade Two of Clausewitz Memorial Public School, where the teacher, Second Lieutenant Mamie Throstlewhistle, is correcting essays on "How I Spent My Summer Vacation."

One child has written of his two weeks as warhead polisher at a missile site; another about the hydrogen bomb he had tried to make in the basement (no bomb, but, on the other hand, no basement any more, either); a third about a visit to U.S. Strategic Air Command, where he was briefed on bombing civilian populations. Little Willie Funk, who is backward, has spent his summer shooting at squirrels with a bow-and-arrow. Miss Throstlewhistle frowns at this and makes a note to set him back a grade unless he does well in assembly and disassembly of the Honest John.

But on the whole she is pleased and in a moment she rises and signals to the class to do the same. Tapping three times on the edge of the desk with her swagger stick, she leads them in singing the school song of Clausewitz Memorial. It is called simply "Fight, Fight, Fight."

Clausewitz, we love you, for you've taught us all we know,
Clausewitz, we'll think of you with every flame we throw,
With every atom bomb we drop, with every shell we fire,
To bring you honour, Clausewitz, shall be our one desire;
Whenever we shall fight a war, we're sure to do it right,
For, Clausewitz, you've taught us how to fight, fight, fight.

Rickety rax, rickety rax,
We're the boys to give 'em whacks,
Masters of ship and tank and plane
Dealers are we in death and pain,
Nothing that kills will we disdain,
Yea-h-h-h, Clausewitz.

Long will we remember all our happy moments here,
The siren calling us to school; at four, the gay all-clear;
The classes in the bomb-proof rooms, the fox-holes in the lawn,
Manœuvres where the shells were real, the armed patrols at dawn.

5

We'll long remember, Clausewitz, the use you've taught of might,
For, Clausewitz, you've taught us how to fight, fight, fight.
Yea-h-h-h, Clausewitz.

And, yea-h-h-h, *Large Soviet Encyclopædia,* Volume 19, Canada.

Yea-h-h-h, humanity.

When it comes to sadism
the place to come is here

One day the United States Senate subcommittee on juvenile delinquency heard about a TV producer who wrote a memo bemoaning the sameness of the executions performed in a television series.

"I like the idea of sadism," he wrote an assistant, "but I hope we can come up with another approach to it."

By curious chance, Congress at the same time was recoiling, as if from some bestiality, from the Administration's proposals for a scheme which would provide medical insurance for the aged as part of Social Security. Better dead than half-way down the slippery slope to socialism, the American Medical Association was saying; or something like that. All of which brings us to the commercial.

If there is a politically-minded television producer about town still looking for something fresh in the sadism line, it so happens that there is a trifle at hand which is available for next season's use for the merest pittance.

[We open on the doorway of a typical suburban home where a woman, fighting back tears, awaits her husband. He speaks.]

"What's the matter, honey?"

"You know I try not to bother you with things, Fred, but you've got to speak to Elwood. He said something today, a simply dreadful thing. Have I been a bad mother to him, Fred? Have I, Fred? Have I?"

"Maude, you know you haven't. Now what was it he said?"

"He said—he said—Fred, I can't tell you, Fred; I know it's going to hurt you. He—said—'What the hell's so terrible about socialized medicine?' "

"Elwood—said—that? Our son? Maude, it makes me feel all empty inside. Where have we gone wrong? I've tried to be a pal to him; Little League and all that. Send him in to me in the study, Maude. In a minute, when I've had a chance to get hold of myself."

[Son enters. Father puts an arm around his shoulders and draws the boy to him.]

"What's this I've been hearing about you, son? About something you said to your mother?"

"All I said was I'd been reading about the American Medical Association and the medicare plan, and all I said was 'What's wrong with socialized medicine anyway,' that's all."

"Boy, don't talk that way. If you have no respect for your parents, for heaven's sake think of the John Birch Society!"

[Rises and crosses to shut window.]

"You getting this in school, son? Man to man, you can tell me. Some Social Science teacher filling your head with this Commie talk? Give it to me straight, son."

"I've just been thinking, that's all. Like it seems I'm not sure about things. Like standing firm; everybody keeps saying we've got to stand firm, like on trade with Cuba. What's that mean?"

"You're not questioning that, are you son? We've got our boys Over There, all over the world; they aren't talking like that. You want to see Old Glory hauled down in the Panama Canal Zone? Viet Nam? One backward step and the whole thing comes down like a pack of cards. If you've been reading, son, it hasn't been Joe Alsop, and that's for sure."

"But we're in favour of negotiating differences. If you negotiate, don't you have to sort of deal? I mean, is negotiating standing firm? and if it isn't. . . ?"

"You're too young to understand these things, son. You can stand firm firmly, and you can stand firm flexibly, see? But first, before you can stand firm flexibly, you've got to stand firm firmly so they don't get the idea you're flexible."

"Well, what about like General de Gaulle? He's so firm he won't even sit down with the Russians to talk about disarmament, like we're doing, but we say he's too flexible because he's going to sell tractors to Cuba."

"That's the way the Communist conspiracy works, son; bores from within. You know how many votes the Commies poll in France? That de Gaulle's a crypto-Communist, Elwood; a pinko.

7

And you take Britain; socialized medicine a few years ago, now they're selling buses to Cuba."

"Still there are some things I don't see. Like, how about China and the United Nations? How can we keep them out?"

"You're talking about Red China, Elwood? Commie China? You know what you're saying?"

"I was just asking. Like the UN isn't ours, is it? It's not like as if they wanted to join the State Department Recreation Association. If most of the members decided maybe the question ought to be disposed of, wouldn't we. . . ?"

"Son, that's Red China you're talking about."

"Well, what I can't see is. . . ."

[Father goes to desk and removes pistol from drawer. There is a shot and the study door bursts open.]

"Fred, you haven't. . . ?"

"It was for the best, Maude; he was rotten, Maude, rotten clean through."

You can tell a Commie plumber by his left-hand Stillson wrench

One day an FBI agent turned up on the doorstep of a Washington home, presented his credentials to the startled woman of the house, and, after a brief all-I-want-is-the-facts-ma'am introduction, asked her if she could tell him anything about a boy who had lived in the neighbourhood ten years earlier. The woman said she hadn't lived in the neighbourhood one year, far less ten, and asked him what was the purpose of this laggard-seeming investigation, anyway. He said the boy was now an applicant for the Peace Corps.

Because of the manifest impossibility of living with a woman whose curiosity is aflame to know what J. Edgar Hoover might hope to uncover while making inquiries about a child, her spouse subsequently put certain questions to the Peace Corps and the FBI. Turned out that a Peace Corps candidate, who may have belonged to a Commie Wolf Cub Pack, or hidden Das Kapital between the covers of his Uncle Wiggily book, is going to be unmasked for the little rotter that he is before he gets many steps beyond the recruiting desk. The FBI said that neighbourhood investigations are part of

8

some security checks. They are intended to find if the candidate was ever in trouble; if his family was well regarded in the community; if he had given any indication of emotional instability in youth.

The FBI man supposed several sets of circumstances in youth concerning which information would be germane to a decision on the person's reliability as an adult. Suppose he had stolen a car. Or suppose he had an elder brother who was active in Communist groups (even though the candidate himself might have rejected the brother's philosophy). Or suppose there had been some story of homosexual practices at, say, a camp, which had involved the youth.

"Of course," said the FBI man, "the reports we make are non-evaluatory. The agency makes the decisions."

A spokesman for the Peace Corps said that the FBI had the job of making security clearances, but the Corps itself, by psychiatric and other tests, assured itself of the stability of all those it accepted. That seemed to put the FBI back to the job of finding out if the applicant, at ten, had been a Commie.

Obviously, when the Peace Corps sends a young man out to teach plumbing to the people of Upper Volta, he is a politically sound, emotionally well-adjusted young man. He may also be a good plumber.

It can be counted a blessing that Ivan IV hadn't TV, too

Ivan the Terrible (né Ivan Ivanovich), we have been told, had a neurotic strain in his character.

This is a diagnosis which would seem to be amply supported if there were nothing to go on but the well-authenticated fact that, while still in his teens, he threw one of his boyars to his dogs. This *could* have been a simple case of a teen-ager being destructive, as presumably they were in his time (1530-1584) as well, but, if so, his rebellion against authority could be said to have taken an advanced form.

In any event, he threw the boyar to the dogs. This was an act which ingratiated him to the numerous people who had been oppressed by the boyars, and presumably to the dogs, but did not endear him

9

to the boyars as a class. (A *boyar,* to benefit those of you who may
not have studied the matter intensively, was a member of a peculiar
order of the old Russian aristocracy next in rank to a *knyaz.* The
old Russian aristocracy went to the dogs wholesale somewhat later,
but that is another story.)

So much for that.

Now we are told by Mikhail Gerasimov, a noted Soviet anthro-
pologist-sculptor, that a study of Ivan's bones suggests that what
sent him into his rages was actually back-ache.

So we now know that Ivan had a neurotic strain and that he
had a bad back. When we add to that that he was overweight, had
big eyes, a low forehead, an underslung jaw, and five wives (although not at once), we see that Ivan was—well, he had some
very difficult adjustments to make.

Nevertheless, Gerasimov's theory that it was the back-ache
that caused Ivan to dispose of people—which he did, sometimes
by the round dozen—still does not reveal sufficient motivation. And
it is here that we think we have some contribution to make to science.
It seems entirely possible, probable, one might even say, that, along
with the airplane, the telephone, and the copper pot, the commercial
was invented in Russia.

Ivan IV, as he became, is *known* to have been much closer to
the merchant class than to the boyars, understandably, in the circumstances perhaps; but the point is that if the hard-sell was developed
in Russia, Ivan could hardly have avoided being exposed to it.

Does the situation begin to come clear? There he was, a man
with a slight neurotic strain, a bad back, an underslung jaw, and five
wives, and no escape, or none short of mayhem, from the shrill cries
of the hucksters telling him that relief was just a swallow away. Is it
to be wondered that he became Terrible?

> One morning when Ivan arose from his pad,
> He felt very far from his best;
> His stomach was logey, his eye was quite red,
> He had a most terrible throb in his head,
> And just at that moment a voice near him said:
>
>> *Do you suffer from dull, nagging back-ache,*
>> *sleepless nights, that dragged-out feeling?*
>
> He took out his sword and he said, "You'll be glad
> To hear that I'm also depressed;
> And when I'm depressed, I'm inclined to be gruff,

I'm vicious, I'm mean and I'm frightfully tough,
And of you and commercials I've had quite enough,"
—And he cut the poor blighter down dead.

Well, now, who's to blame him? Who among us, in fact, has not at times wanted to indulge his slight neurotic strain the same way? We are told that up until 1550, when he was twenty, Ivan's private life was abominable. In that year, however, he straightened up—morally, of course; physically, his back continued to kill him—and for ten years he ruled in a somewhat enlightened way.

In 1570, however, things began to bug him again and . . . . But there is an old Russian tale that has come down the centuries that tells it better than anyone today could hope to do:

One day when the cares of the world bore him down,
He found it a chore to get dressed;
His mind was lethargic, his outlook was blue,
His aches were much greater than anyone knew,
And just at that moment a group chose to do:

Do you suffer the excruciating pain of
rheumatism, arthritis or neuralgia? Well—

He drew himself up and he frowned a black frown,
And he said, "Might I merely suggest,
That you run a great risk when I'm feeling unwell
In coming before me with nostrums to sell
For I wish with great fervour to see you in hell,"
—And dispatched that whole unctuous crew.

And so it went, year after year; here a chop, there a chop, everywhere a chop-chop. Snick, plop, and another Russian bit the dust.

One evening when Ivan was awkwardly bent,
He hobbled quite plainly distressed;
His tongue was all coated, his cheek was dead pale,
His mood was most rancid, embittered and stale,
And just then another let out a low wail:

Is the wrong mattress robbing you of your
proper night's rest?

And Ivan rose up and said, "I'm a gent
Who by demons is sometimes possessed;
I know that I'm touchy, irascible, yes,
And rather quick tempered you'd think me, I guess,

11

But I hope you will pardon this latest excess,"
—And he rent him from wish-bone to tail.

And that is why Ivan was Terrible and commercials have been terrible ever since.

So if you don't like it here
get your own etcetera market

> Most stores still operate on the antiquated system which requires a customer to stand in line to choose the item he wants, then get in another line to pay the cashier for the item, and then take the receipt back to the original counter and pick up the goods. This can make even buying a pair of shoelaces a half-hour experience.
>
> —Moscow correspondent in the
> *Washington Evening Star*

Dear Vladimir:

I have been here in capital of United States for two weeks and am enjoying very much. I live not very far out and I can walk downtown in twenty minutes, but if I have time I take the bus.

They have no subway here like ours, only buses, which are very big, but not many. What I am told is that in capitalist society all people have cars and they drive to work because the buses are so few. The buses are so few because there are not enough people to use them.

When so many people drive to work the roads, called "means of access" (what is?), quickly become inadequate. When they are improved, more people drive to work, and the bus system becomes even worse, and because of that more people drive to work, and the means of access have to be improved. This I think does not make sense but that is the way they do it.

But it was the stores I wanted to tell you about. In the big stores, like our GUM, most trading is done with what are called "charge plates." Some people still use money, but the people who work in the stores do not like this and when they are handed money they will say, "You don't have a charge account?" in an accusing way. The

12

managements like their customers to have charge accounts because then they will buy more than they can afford and will have to work harder to get the money to pay for these goods, which will be worn out by then. The people who work in the stores do not like to handle money because then they have to give change, and this takes away from the time they have for things like picking their teeth.

You will have heard of the famous drugstores in the United States, but you will not know that one, downtown here in the very capital, one time had Lee-Enfield rifles for sale in its front window. It is a strange business.

There is one retail store in downtown Washington which has a system like ours where the customer chooses the item he wants, goes to the cashier to pay for the item, and then takes the receipt back to the original coounter to pick up the goods. It is a liquor store and the service is very efficient. I believe the power structure wants the lower classes to drink so as to keep them tractable.

Most food stores still operate on an antiquated system which requires the customer to go and get his own things and put them in a cart (telejka) which he pushes around in front of him. It is very funny and also very tiring because the food stores are very large and everything is spread all around. There is never anyone to say where anything is, and if you do find someone in a white coat and say, "Where are kept the prunes?" he usually will reply, "They must be around somewhere; I don't work here regular, I just come in on Saturdays." This is very confusing, especially on Fridays. I think these are people who are kept in work-camps the rest of the week, for they are very surly in their manner.

These places are called "super markets." We would call them warehouses (sklad) rather than markets, but this I think I understand. Super, I do not understand. An American dictionary says "super, colloq., a shortened form of superintendent," but this I do not think can be. It also says super means "extremely fine, great, etc.," and I suppose this is the meaning, because certainly they are full of etcetera.

The managers of these etcetera markets are very clever and they understand very well the mind of the American woman, which is not strong. In these etcetera markets all of the goods are put out on the shelves, because the American woman never knows what she is shopping for until she sees it.

It is for this same reason that the meat counter is always put at

13

the place farthest away from the door, so that the women will have to go past the greatest number of shelves, and will buy things they hadn't come in for. At the meat counter everything is already wrapped in packages which have cellophane on one side and a piece of cardboard on the other. The side with the cardboard on it is the side which has the bone and fat. Also at the meat counter there is a button and a sign which says, "If you don't see what you want, ring bell." But nobody ever answers; or if someone does, he says they have not got any.

There are many lines: lines to get through the aisles, which are always narrow so the women shoppers will pass close to things which they then will buy; lines at the meat counter and the bakery counter (they do not have bread in this country but something which is made of old bath sponges wrapped in damp brown paper); but the biggest line of all is the one everyone has to get in to get out. There are several of these, but the management has it arranged that whichever one you are in is the slow one.

Any time that buying a pair of shoelaces is a half-hour experience is counted a good day by the people.

Fraternally,

IVAN

Not just any damp candidate accepted by State Department

It now looks as if occasional bed-wetting isn't going to keep anyone from getting a job as a code-clerk in the United States Department of State.

This unfortunate failing reigned as an undeniable hazard to employment until David A. Belisle, a security officer in the department, quietly withdrew a psychological test which had been in use for less than a month.

But it was too much to hope that withdrawal could keep quiet a test which asked applicants if they sometimes wet the bed, or had problems of any kind with their sex-life—an invitation, God wot, to all sorts of lurid reminiscences—or if they perspired for no good reason. What, surely, would give anyone good reason for perspiring,

14

copiously, was the test itself. It ran to thirteen pages. Applicants were told it might take one to five hours to complete. And they were warned not to seek advice in answering ("Do I wet the bed, dear?" "Yes, I'm afraid you do.")

> Not every single Secretary's brightly intellectual;
> Assistants often serve for years though wholly ineffectual,
> And many men have done their terms in posts ambassadorial
> Who wouldn't know an aide mémoire from leading editorial.
> Diplomacy does not disbar the nastily acidulous,
> And men have often served abroad though frankly rather bibulous;
> To all of these positions those with failings may aspire
> —But you cannot be a code-clerk if you needlessly perspire.

Mr. Belisle said the tests were for medical information and had nothing to do with security, an assurance that was oddly welcome. The thought that the State Department might be worried about the security aspects of fingernail-biting, or laughing while asleep, leads to some wild fantasies. For instance:

A pale shaken little man sits under a spotlight, five agents of a Foreign Power in a circle around him. One of them speaks: "Hokay, Fotheringill, the code. We-want-the-code. We're through being easy with you. Either we get it or tomorrow the world knows you for what you are—a fingernail-biter."

[Terrified cries of, "No, no; not that!"]

Or, perhaps: "The jig's up, Fotheringill. We're prepared to unmask you for the bed-wetter that you are."

[Fotheringill faints dead away.]

The quiz also asked prospective code-clerks how they got along with their wives, and, "Explain any sources of conflict in your marital life. (If none, what factors contribute to promoting harmony?)" There was in this, of course, the clear implication that if the candidate could not produce some substantial evidence of conflict, he had better be prepared to clear himself of the suspicion of being mealy-mouthed and untrustworthy.

The quiz also asked applicants if they were ever tired or run down, and if they depended on medicines, sedatives or laxatives.

> Officials aren't required to swear to lives of sweet
> tranquility,
> Nor owning nerves possessing less than normal
> frangibility,

15

And if their dreams are filled with things all vilely
    fanged and hideous,
They're not required to make this known for use perhaps
    invidious;
Diplomacy is thus revealed as not unduly quizzical
To find its topmost people's faults, the mental and
    the physical,
But still the lowly code-clerk must establish it's a fact
That he's not the one for purges of his alimentary tract.

Applicants were asked how often and to what extent they felt tense or keyed up; whether they ever had difficulty falling asleep or staying asleep; if they were restless, jumpy, jittery and couldn't seem to sit still; and if things sometimes appeared strange, peculiar, unnatural or unreal. (Candidates who thought the test appeared strange, peculiar, unnatural and unreal presumably were prudent not to say so.)

They were asked if their hands trembled, or if they feared crowds, heights, water, places, or needles. Goodness knows why needles.

A strange dislike of needles very seldom would be critical
In saying who would get the post of French Affairs
    (Political);
A tendency, if kept in bounds, to bouts of saturnalia,
Would rarely bar a man's being sent as envoy to Australia;
And furthermore the very thought is laughably erroneous
That married life of diplomats is never inharmonious;
There's that tolerance of weakness when it touches
    those ahead
—But you cannot be a code-clerk if you sometimes wet
    the bed.

It gives one to think.

Twinkle, twinkle DAR
how I wonder what you are

Along with the celebrated cherry blossoms, spring brings to Washington the Daughters of the American Revolution, a sort of collective Major-General Edwin A. Walker in a blue rinse and a hat with daisies on it. From all around the country the Daughters flock into Constitution Hall, where they roost for a week, happily saluting the last revolution and standing on guard against the next.

If there is one thing the Daughters are not—and there certainly is—it is changeable. Thus, when you've seen one DAR convention, you've seen 'em all: a great conclave of ample, motherly women in white dresses with sashes, occupied with such motherly concerns as whether or not the country is sufficiently supplied with rich, nourishing A-bombs.

The Daughters are given to passing resolutions which expose Fabian socialism for the insidious menace that it is, and taking a dear-old-grey-haired-mother-of-mine view of disarmament, namely "Nuts to that!" These are the girls who believe in having something put by for a rainy day; a handful of Minuteman missiles, for instance. When they invite a man to speak to them, they lean to the sort of men who have their own keen-eyed awareness of the lurking peril.

On one occasion when their annual manœuvres were attended by a foreign observer, they had as one speaker Senator Strom Thurmond, or Senator Thurm Stromond, as one be-sashed Daughter called him, a man who is so wide-awake to the Communist menace that he's a virtual political insomniac. Another speaker at that same conclave was Admiral Arleigh Burke, the former Naval Chief of Staff, a sailor with a pronounced starboard list.

The Daughters, as they call themselves, are affected by J. Edgar Hoover as some of their less steely sisters used to be affected by Liberace. Not that they squeal, God forbid, but there is a definite impression in the hall of hard breathing.

"Madam Chairman," said one, apropos of goodness knows what, "may I take it that every one of you admires J. Edgar Hoover and the work of his organization?"

She could. The Daughters responded in J. Edgar Hoover fanclub fashion. A moment later another was declaring that she was sure "from that fine applause of the name of J. Edgar Hoover, that the Daughters of the American Revolution admire this fine man."

"Fine" is an in-word with the DAR. "Wonderful" is another. As, for instance, ". . . we want to get this fine (anti-Communist) literature to the wonderful youth of this country."

The Daughters were discussing whether or not—and it was early apparent it was going to be not—to give $60,000 to Freedom's Foundation, an organization also engaged in protecting the American heritage, constitution, way of life, etc., from the depredations of evil-intentioned or merely misdirected persons, within and without. It wasn't that Freedom's Foundation wasn't a fine organization doing wonderful work, but that the DAR ought to spend its own money. J. Edgar Hoover's place in it never became precisely clear to one observer, but it was evident from the applause that there was a large measure of support for the point of view advanced by one delegate:

"If we want to give an award to J. Edgar Hoover we can give it as Daughters of the American Revolution."

Another struck to the heart of the matter with a reference to a great bane of the DAR, foreign aid.

"I have loved the way we have stood against foreign aid, the principle of foreign aid," she said. "And this is the same thing, giving it to others when we need it ourselves."

A Hawaiian delegate, who said that fighting communism was very dear to her, was otherwise minded. And, as she told her sisters in a so-there voice, her state had more powerful Communists than the mainland states. The woman who had trouble with Admiral Burt and Senator Thurm Stromond asked severely if the Daughters assembled thought that these fine men would be in anything that wasn't truly American, seemingly the Foundation in dispute.

Nobody seemed to think that, and the Daughters moved on to the reading of the resolutions which said, among other things, that the United States Arms Control and Disarmament agency should be shut up post-haste, and "the sovereign right of self-defense inherent in every sovereign state" should be reasserted. It was probably those eight hundred-odd ICBM's and the couple of thousand long-range bombers that had misled most people to believe that it was being asserted.

Other resolutions gave the back of the DAR's hand to medical care for the aged under Social Security, the Post Office (for allowing Communist literature to pass through the mails), the Common Market, Fabian socialism, and restrictions on military brass hats from speaking out on anything, any time.

The DAR may be against quite a lot, but it's for J. Edgar Hoover, and any girl who is for J. Edgar Hoover can't be all bad.

18

Soviet speaks with forked tongue
red man orbits great iron bird

You've got to fight fire with fire, I always say; and mighty tiresome I make myself with it, too. But back in the days when the Russians were short of scientific achievements of their own, they had a way of appropriating other people's. Blandly they told the world that the telephone, the airplane and sundry other devices were inventions of sons of Mother Russia.

There was an incomparable opportunity to borrow the technique and put it to good use the day that Yuri Gagarin went hurtling around the earth, leaving the West open-mouthed and very, very much behind.

The plot was this:

Gagarin, we were told, translates into English as Wild Duck. What the United States Information Agency needed to do was to put it about that the cosmonaut's square name was Wild Duck, and that Gagarin was simply the Russian translation. This maybe will provide some inkling of what we're getting at:

> By the shores of broad Lake Huron,
> Hard against the daunting forest,
> Stood the home of William Wild Duck;
> Mighty Hunter William Wild Duck,
> Out in front there stood a cradle,
> Stood the cradle of the boy-child,
> Stood the nest of little Yuri*;
> From the forest came a gypsy,
> Came on stealthy feet a gypsy,
> Came an ill-intentioned gypsy.

> > To the cradle sped this felon
> > There to snatch the sleeping infant,
> > Snatch him from his bed of rushes,
> > Snatch him from his parents' keeping,
> > Etc., etc., etc.

You begin to get the picture? Actually, Gagarin is an Ojibway Indian, scion of one of North America's oldest families, kidnapped

---

* William Wild Duck was a mighty hunter, all right, but a lousy speller. He thought he'd registered the kid's birth under the name of Howard.

in infancy by a Romanian gypsy. Everybody knows where the Romanians stand, ideology-wise.

So the kid grew up behind the Iron Curtain, a model youth in every way, except for occasions when he'd get a faraway look in his eyes and take to wearing feathers in his hair. He was really a free-enterpriser at heart, and wanted to set up in the beaded moccasin business. When this cosmonaut thing came along, he put his name down for it.

And now, as we prepare to blast off, once more it's "over to you, Henry Wadsworth Longfellow*."

> High above he soared in orbit,
> Soared all weightless in his space ship,
> Saw our planet far beneath him,†
> Saw whole oceans, mountains, rivers,
> Saw at last a certain forest
> Standing dark beside the water;
> Saw a half-remembered wigwam,
> Felt the tug of distant memory,
> Heard the call of ancient voices.

Get it? The kid was going to land back at the old reservation, by the shores of broad Lake Huron, hard against the daunting forest, but when he got overhead he couldn't get his flaps down. So, perforce, he returned to Russia, taking with him shattered dreams of freedom and owning his own beaded moccasin business. It's a touching tale, and supposing only a quarter of the Afro-Asians go for it—well, a quarter's better than nothing.

At home a veritable harvest of headlines could be foreseen:

FIRST ASTRONAUT NATIVE AMERICAN

OJIBWAY ORBITS OLD ORB

SHARP NOTE TO MOSCOW
SEEKS ON-SITE INSPECTION
OF ASTRONAUT WILD DUCK

KHRUSHCHEV TELLS U.S.
AHHH! BLAST OFF

* Henry Wadsworth Longfellow (1807-1882) wrote a large number of poems presumably to have them parodied. He must have had something in mind.
† It is an interesting physiological note, gleaned from one's perfunctory studies of aero-medicine years ago, that flying at extreme heights is often conducive to discomforting flatulence. At two hundred miles up it must be a brute.

There's no telling what might have come of it. Khrushchev might have been so chagrined he'd have beaten his missiles into ploughshares, and spent the rest of his life deflowering the virgin lands, or whatever it is the Russians do to virgin lands.

Meanwhile, back at the Henry Wadsworth Longfellow:

> Many medals Khrushchev gave him,
> Strung his aching breast with ribbons,
> Tendered him the city's freedom,*
> Tendered him a great reception;
> Fond admirers flocked about him,
> Called him Star of All the Heavens,
> Still his eye remained beclouded,
> Still his heart was filled with yearning,
> Yearning for the distant teepee,†
> Yearning for the reservation.

Poignant? Almost insupportably so. Far-fetched? Oh, I don't know. Compared with that confection about the U-2 and the weather flight, it doesn't look bad.

OK, Ivan, if you've got the key let's have the Politburo Polka

It was Gerd Wilcke, a correspondent of *The New York Times* in Bonn, who was responsible for the intelligence that the East Germans had taken to livening things up with state-approved songs. Mr. Wilcke gave several samples, the catchiest of which went like this:

> Heidi of the chicken farm,
> All the boys, from near and far,
> Like you as do the chickens
> All the chickens love their feeds
> And as reward, with daily egg the norm they meet.

It is to be hoped that it will not be considered narrow partisanship if one ventures the view that that last line leaves a little some-

---

* Such as it is.
† You can take the boy out of the teepee, but can you take the teepee out of the boy? *Old Ojibway saying*

thing to be desired. Possibly the verse suffered in the translation. In any case, this is an area of the Cold War that the West cannot let go by default. Nor does it need to. By pure good fortune, it happens that there is at hand a song about another Heidi, employed not on a chicken farm, but in an industry which, shall we say, is one step up the ladder of technology. It is sung by a young man, a fellow-worker, who is. . . . But let the song tell its own story.

> Dear Heidi, girl of many moods
> Who labours there in frozen foods,
> I hold in awe;
> I love you when your nose is blue,
> Or, when from work, bedecked with dew,
> You gently thaw.

This is a love story in the great Hollywood trodition. It has echoes of Horatio Algae, the Great American Dream, and Mom's (frozen) apple pie—which, incidentally, echoed like a kettle-drum under the fork.

The young man went on:

> Can I, while here condemned to freeze
> These packets of plebeian peas,
> Approach your folks,
> While you, my sweet, earn more per hour
> Entrusted with choice cauliflower
> And artichokes?

And there you have it—just a beginning, you understand—a story of young love in America, of the young man, working, dreaming, striving. It fair chokes you up.

Mr. Wilcke cited a couple of other bits from the East German repertoire, including one that began:

> Man reaches for the stars fulfilling age-old dream,
> Conquers for himself the distant, masters space,
> Man stands on the road leading to. . . .

Pretentious stuff, that. We were rather toying here with something simpler, something that would hit them where they live. Something like:

> Werner von Braun, we salute you,
> We salute you, dear Werner von Braun,
> Your Titan or Redstone, whichever it is,

Has oft to the heights so majestically riz,
And the times that it hasn't, well that's rocket biz,
Werner von Braun, we salute etc., etc.

That "oft" is a nice touch. It gives a verse a spot of class to insert an oft now and again. That and " 'twixt."

But we hurry along. In the battle for men's minds, one must always be on the hop, hop, hop.

Mr. Wilcke also recited a bit of what he called a ballad (every man to his own definition) which went like this:

Red rockets circle the universe;
Carry to the sun, carry to the sun,
Greeting from the Party, and the might
Of Labour hails the Soviet scientist.

Call it professional jealousy if you will, but that one will never replace "Red Sails in the Sunset," or "The Red River Valley," or even that fine old medical school song, "Red Grow the Rashes, O." Not in my affections.

But if it's ballads of accomplishment that the anonymous East German songsmith wants, let him sink his teeth into the following:

There's a wall-oven out in the kitchen,
A freezer that's colder than Nome,
And upstairs, if you hush,
You can just hear the flush,
In the Average American Home.

The car is bedecked and bedizened,
TV is our talk and our tome
And we barbecue steaks
On a spit in two shakes,
In the Average American Home.

There's a thing that digests all the garbage,
Detergents eat dirt in their foam,
The dishwasher rinses
Our plates of their blintzes,
In the Average American Home.

The bathroom's a-gleam with ceramics,
The kitchen's a-glitter with chrome,
And sound has grown chronic
And stereophonic
In the Average American Home.

So, Ivan, put check to your boasting,
Your science has far yet to roam,
When you've shot to the sun
You'll have hardly begun
On the Average American Home.

OTTAWA

Lint from the pant cuffs of history

The national capital; a wise child's guide

The City of Ottawa, which was incorporated in 1855, grew out of the military and construction camp which served as headquarters for the building of the Rideau Canal between 1826 and 1832. Even today it looks as if it hadn't grown out of it completely.

The City is extremely well favoured by nature, being located on the Ottawa River where the Rideau flows into it from the one side and the Gatineau from the other. In Ottawa, however, the North American genius for misuse, defacement and obliteration of natural beauty has been brought to one of its highest states of development. It was in 1857, ten years before Confederation, that Queen Victoria selected Ottawa to be the seat of government. But for this circumstance, Parliament Hill, a magnificent green promontory overlooking the Ottawa River, undoubtedly would be given over today to a trailer camp or an amusement park.

This is not to say that Ottawa is without beauty. Beauty is to be found for the most part in places—the driveways, for example—where land has been liberated by the Federal government from the withering hand of a municipal authority which, on the evidence available, has historically pursued blight with the single-minded dedication with which a lecher pursues blondes. Neither is it to say that steps are not being taken to *improve* the national capital—not so many steps nor so enthusiastically taken as those to create more ugliness, perhaps— but some.

Plans for the improvement of Ottawa have had a sorry history. In 1913 a Federal Planning Commission was created and told to prepare a comprehensive plan. This was done, but fortunately World War I intervened before it became necessary to do anything about it, and nothing ever was. In 1922 another plan was prepared but, in that same year, Kemal Ataturk drove the Greeks into the sea at Smyrna and demanded the evacuation of Eastern Thrace; and that plan came to nothing, too.

27

In 1937 the Federal government, anticipating the probable onset of another war in Europe, invited the noted French city planner, Jacques Greber, to come to Ottawa to replan the city centre. The Government's prescience shortly was confirmed, and there was only time to dedicate the new memorial to the *last* war in Confederation Square before the next war began.

M. Greber was invited to return to Ottawa in 1945, by which time the first essential of improvement was the immediate retention of the services of a skilled arsonist. M. Greber, nevertheless, did his best. This time he was asked to prepare a master plan for the development of, not just Ottawa, but a national capital district which would encompass nine hundred square miles and both the communities of Ottawa and Hull. Two considerations lay behind the choice of this more ambitious plan:

1. Canada had emerged from World War II physically unscathed and relatively rich. Now the modest improvement plans which had been procrastinated over before no longer seemed suitable to a great nation, and it was decided that a much grander concept would have to be adopted to procrastinate over.

2. Since another war did not seem likely to present itself immediately as an excuse for doing nothing at all, it was decided that the effort should be as diffuse as possible, so that it would not show. One reason for this was the desire to avoid giving alarm to native Ottawans, who are as sensitive as they are complacent. (Ottawans customarily react to any word of criticism of the national capital with shrill cries of "Well, what's so hot about Toronto?" Or Winnipeg, or Calgary, or Halifax. The obvious answer is that there is nothing hot about these places; each is its own shame, whereas Ottawa is the nation's shame. One of the troubles that beset the national capital is that Ottawans treat it as if they own it, and most other Canadians treat it as if they don't.

In the twenty years since M. Greber's second coming, work on his plan has proceeded at a pace to ensure not only that the peace of mind of the natives will be undisturbed, but also that the portions undertaken first will be ready for demolition by the time the last are completed. To say that its execution is being pressed half-heartedly would be only to praise torpor with faint damns.

The centre, the heart of Ottawa, is, of course, Parliament Hill. In addition to the Parliament buildings, and the unobstructed view they afford of the toilet-tissue works of the E. B. Eddy Company, Parliament Hill is notable for a lovers' walk on the riverside hill face. For many years now, this walk has been closed and the public warned off with signs, in case it should provide opportunities for a particular sort of immorality, immorality on Parliament Hill having been restricted to sorts that may be committed in the vertical plane.

The river view from Parliament Hill provides a constant reminder of Ottawa's past as a lumbering centre. There, just across the river in Quebec, are the Eddy Company's vast piles of pulp wood which, by some cruel misfortune, have never caught fire and burned down that monumental eyesore, the bridge that connects Ottawa with Hull. (The view in the other direction from Parliament Hill takes in the Rideau Club, which is also filled with dead wood that has never caught fire.)

In the great days of wooden ships, timbers for them passed through the national capital. Ottawa sent Irishmen up the river and got back timbers, which not only made a profitable commercial enterprise but a fair exchange. Giant white pines came down the river for masts, and those that were marked seconds, or mill rejects, were bought by the municipal corporation to be put up as light, telegraph and telephone poles. And there they stand on most of Ottawa's streets to this day, leaning drunkenly over the roadways, and festooned with wires . . . so as to cover the sky over downtown Ottawa with one endless cat's-cradle. Ottawa children have grown to manhood not knowing that the whole world does not exist under some sort of net.

It tells something about Ottawa that the one thing which its residents unfailingly point out about their city is that it is easy to get out of. When they want to be good, they go across the river to swim and ski in the Gatineau Hills. When they want to be bad they go to Montreal. And when they die, all of those who have not made it in life hope to go to Rockcliffe.

Rockcliffe is a self-governing tax haven within the boundaries of Ottawa, on its east side. It is the Establishment ghetto, and is populated by members of the Cabinet, senior civil servants, diplomats, newspaper publishers, successful merchants, investment counsellors, lawyers and lobbyists, all of those in the first seven categories from time to time overlapping with the eighth. It is a community of light industry, the principal products of which are the Martini and the Smoked Salmon Canapé. The highest aspiration of its people is Not To Be Confused With Ottawans; its sin is sleeping with one another's ideas. Hunting the Wily Status is a favoured Ottawa sport. City people frequently pursue the elusive Status into Rockcliffe only to

29

find it has gone to ground in the Senate, a half-dozen Rockcliffians howling after it.

A large part of the reason why so much of the City of Ottawa looks like hell—or like Hull, for that matter, which is even worse—is that so many people who think of themselves as Community Leaders, in capital letters, have immured themselves in the Village of Rockcliffe Park. They take their livings from the city, and their municipal services at less cost than would be possible if the village provided its own, and they give back the waste of their drains, but not demonstrably much else.

The architecture of Rockcliffe is mostly what is called, in England, Stockbroker Tudor, but it is giving way more and more, in new building, to California Contemptible. This merely reflects the general change that has been taking place in a national taste which, unswervingly derivative, increasingly finds its highest ideals expressed in the plumbing ads of *Better Homes and Gardens,* rather than in the estate sales advertisements in *Country Life,* as once was the case.

The architecture of most of the new suburban subdivisions of Ottawa proper consists of expanses of NHA Tedium broken here and there by examples of Outright Atrocity. In seeking decentralization, the Federal government has created in Tunney's Pasture and Confederation Heights two complexes of buildings of a style which a kindly critic has described as Office Blocks Anonymous. In fact, had they been committed by the Canadian government outside the confines of Canada, a motion of censure on the ground of cultural aggression unquestionably could have been made to carry the United Nations General Assembly.

Ottawa is known as a city where people dine and entertain at home, ostensibly because they find their pleasure in good talk and the exchange of ideas. The actual explanation is that a cuisine running extensively to grilled cheese sandwiches and fried scallops must soon deter even the most determined out-goer.

There is no national theatre in the nation's capital, and no building to put it in if there were. Those troupes of wandering minstrels which occasionally stumble upon Ottawa by mischance, or by the malevolence of some ill-disposed booking agent, are called upon to perform in temples erected to the genius of Mickey Mouse. Apart from that, it is all church basements. This is about to be corrected with the building of a National Centre of the Performing Arts—about, of course, being an uncertain term. (It took about thirty years to complete the acquisition of the piece of land on which has been

30

erected a Garden of the Provinces, a sort of Forest Lawn for Confederation.) Once the centre is completed, there will remain only the task of finding some performing arts to put in it, perhaps including the orchestra which languished in bitterness and bitterly died.

There *is* a National Gallery of Art which, by blind luck, is located where an art gallery ought to be located—smack downtown where people can drop in casually, at noon, or whenever the prevailing awfulness drives them to seek refuge. This, of course, is to be changed. The gallery in time will be moved to a less central location, although the glacial pace at which all programmes proceed fairly ensures that the stroke of inadvertent wisdom which put the gallery where it is will not be undone for several generations.

Some years ago, the City of Ottawa adopted a new coat of arms, replacing an appropriately cluttered old set which displayed, among many other symbols, a Junoesque Justice (blindfolded) facing a moody-looking blacksmith, a sheaf of wheat, a disembodied arm wielding a hatchet, a hive of bees, a plough, a railway locomotive, two stags beside a lake at sundown, a set of locks on the Rideau River, a waterfall with a bridge and two men fishing from a row-boat, and a large gear hanging in mid-air at about the blacksmith's knees. The new arms are simpler, including notably a white pine tree, and, set in it in a little circle, an oak tree, the whole described as "a white pine tree fructed proper charged with a bezant thereon an oak tree eradicated and fructed also proper;" and a shield. The shield is divided into four parts, in the upper left of which is a crown, and in the lower right a maple leaf. The other two sections have been left blank, indicating, as the City itself said at the time, that "Ottawa's real greatness lies before her, and is still to be realized."

Shall we pray?

And *then there's that one*
oh, say can you see, by the . . .

WANT AD: Old patriotic songs refurbished while you wait. Satisfaction guaranteed or your $1,000 back.

Let's see now, for $1,000:

> The ump-tee-ump, our em-blem dear,
> The ump-tee-ump, for-ev-er. . . .

When the contest was announced, Gordon V. Thompson, the music publisher, said that one of the things wrong with "The Maple Leaf Forever" was the maple leaf. Apparently the song didn't do anything for a lot of people in the Golden West who had never seen a maple tree. So, obviously, we've got to start by finding something that inspires reverence in the West. It's a pity that "money" has only two syllables. Gophers? Premier Manning? Wheat?

> Northern wheat, our em-blem dear,
> Northern wheat, for-ev-er,
> Oh, bless our soil and Chou En-Lai,
> And Mitchell Sharp for-ev-er.

If that doesn't bring them out of their sod huts cheering, nothing will.

But the chorus can wait; it's time to attack the verse, with (as the instruction goes on the music) spirit.

> In days of yore, from Britain's shore,
> Wolfe the dauntless he-ro came,
> And plan-ted firm Britann-ia's flag
> On Ca-na-da's fair domain.

Hmm!

As the pamphlet describing the contest said, "On account of references to wartime achievements, such as the capture of Quebec, the song is not in harmony with Canada's thinking today."

Especially in Quebec.

Plainly the thing's got to be broadened a bit. Let's see.

> In days of yore, from Britain's shore,
> Wolfe the dauntless he-ro came. . . .

Not even all English-speaking Canadians came from Britain's

32

shore, so that reference is out. As for Wolfe, what with Separatists pushing his monument down the hill at the Plains of Abraham, or whatever, it would seem prudent to drop him. Perhaps as a substitute:

> In days gone by, by sea and sky,
> People came from here and there. . . .

This, it will be noted, takes account of all the postwar immigrants who came to Canada by air—rather a clever stroke, one is moved immodestly to observe. The reference to their coming from here and there is intended to ensure that all, regardless of race or creed (as we liberals like to say) can join in with equal enthusiasm.

> And plan-ted firm Britann-ia's flag
> On Ca-na-da's fair domain.

Obviously something has to be done about that "plan-ted firm Britann-ia's flag." But plan-ted what? Their feet?

> And plan-ted firm their restless feet
> On Ca-na-da's fair domain.

It's hardly inspiring.

> And settled down to make their home
> On Ca-na-da's fair domain.

Better.

> Here may it wave, our boast, our pride,
> And joined in love together,
> The Thistle, Shamrock, Rose entwine
> The Maple Leaf for-ev-er!

Having disposed of Britannia's flag for good and sufficient reason, something necessarily has to replace that "here may it wave," etc. Let's see how we stand now:

> In days gone by, by sea and sky,
> People came from here and there,
> And sett-led down, to make their home
> On Ca-na-da's fair domain.
> By brig and barque, the British came,
> In stately sloop and schooner,
> But they weren't the first to reach these shores,
> —The French had got there sooner.

By George, can't you just see the *habitants* in their toques and

33

sashes, singing, as they dance hand-in-hand around Donald Gordon roasting at the stake, there in Place Ville Marie? It fair brings a lump to the throat.

> The Fleur-de-Lis, our emblem dear,
> The Fleur-de-Lis, for-ev-er,
> The Thistle, Shamrock, Rose entwine
> The Fleur-de-Lis, for-ev-er.

(Western audiences at this point may substitute the chorus about "Number One Northern Hard." Unity does not demand slavish uniformity.)

The Canadian Authors Association is advised to send the cheque to George Bain, 1099 National Press Building, Washington, D.C., 20004.

And, do you know, they never even wrote?

Oh, that national capital it's a fun, fun, fun place

SOCIAL NOTES THAT HAVE BEEN WIDELY OVERLOOKED: It was in a recent election campaign that a candidate, making a surprisingly strong run against a supposedly well-entrenched member, was asked by a reporter what he thought had done him the most political good during the campaign.

"Unquestionably the private tea-parties," said the candidate, without a moment's hesitation. "Since this campaign began, I've been intimate with most of the women in this constituency."

Well, every man to his own sort of campaign.

And then there was the story about a Chief Justice of the Supreme Court of Canada, no less, who became known as a rather too-attentive dinner partner. It was a woman who had suffered an evening with him who subsequently told someone that he made her think of an Indian.

"An Indian?" she was asked.

"Yes," she replied. "He's a Pawnee Chief."

It desperately needs to be added that the jurist in question went to his reward many years ago.

34

The two may be unconnected
but lately they've voted Tory

In his celebrated Royal Commission report on Canada's economic prospects, Walter Gordon suggested that if growth in the Maritimes did not pick up enough, one remedy might be to assist some of the people to move. Mr. Gordon has not made a point of reviving the idea as Minister of Finance.

A TALE OF LOVE IN ACADIA
or
THE SECOND EXPULSION OF THE ACADIANS

These are the ocean provinces; average per capita income
Hard-wrung from sub-marginal farms, grey seas,
    grim mines,
Stands at a lowly level, one-third behind the rest,
Which, boastful of their economic growth, just
    turn away;
Loud from the provincial legislatures, the deep-voiced
    premiers
Speak, and in accents disconsolate, proclaim developmental needs.

You don't know Evangeline? Well, there was this girl, Evangeline Bellefontaine, who lived with her old man, Benedict, in the village of Grand-Pré in the Maritimes. He was very big in the farm line.

Evangeline had flipped over Gabriel, the blacksmith's son, a poor boy. As a matter of fact, blacksmithing being what it was at that time (terrible), Gabriel, all by himself, was doing a lot toward bringing down the average per capita income.

We proceed:

Ye who believe in affection that hopes and endures
    and is patient,
Ye who believe in the beauty and strength of
    a woman's devotion,
List to the mournful tradition still sung by the
    pines of the forest,
List to a tale of love in Acadie, home of the depressed.

That part's pure Longfellow, except for the last word. The way

35

he wrote it, the word was "happy," but then Longfellow hadn't read the Gordon report. Maybe Walter Gordon never read Longfellow, either, but that's another matter. Off we go:

> Somewhat apart from the village and nearer the Moderne motel,
> Benedict Bellefontaine, the wealthiest farmer in the region,
> Dwelt on his mortgaged acres, and with him, directing
>   his household,
> Toothsome Evangeline lived, a doll and that year's
>   Miss Grand-Pré.
> Eminently a cool chick, that maiden of seventeen summers,
> Tall and stacked was she, and fair, a sort of Bluenose
>   Brigitte Bardot,
> Bewitching the louts of the village with a single glance;
> A glance, perhaps, but meaningless, for she had eyes
>   for Gabe alone.
> Stalwart and stately in form was the boy of the blacksmith,
> Black as a flue were his locks, and tanned his cheeks
>   like a boot,
> Nothing disclosing, this side his patches and flatness
>   of pocket,
> He came from a depressed industry in a depressed area.

Doesn't that wrench you? Here were these two good kids, Evangie and Gabe, in love, and they were beset by all sorts of troubles not of their own making. Like Gabe's not being able to get a job.

Dominion-Provincial conferences came, and Dominion-Provincial conferences went, but Acadie still continued to present fewer opportunities than other areas of the country. Well, anyway, Evangeline and Gabriel decided to get married. "What the hell," they asked, "we're human ain't we?" It is on the day of the wedding that our story picks up. *Alors:*

> So the morning passed away. And, lo! with a summons sonorous
> Sounded the word from Ottawa, and over the country it spread;
> Thronging ere long were men with briefs. Elsewhere in the
>   country
> Waited petitioners, strongly to argue their economic views
> Oft-times conflicting, illogical, or monotonously repetitive,
> And from out the mass and muddle there came in time reports;
> Then up rose the Commander and spoke from his place in
>   the House
> Holding aloft in his hands, with seals thereon affixed,
> The fat, grey-clad product of his Royal Commission.

You get the picture? These kids are about to get married and the Government sends out a Royal Commission which, as we have seen, has submitted its report. Can this document have any meaning for them? Will their marriage plans be affected? Will New Brunswick get assistance with its Hydro bonds? Read on, read on:

"The fact remains," said the report, "that the Atlantic Provinces,
Old though they may be and gracious, continue to trail the rest."
Thereupon it suggested curatives, some benign, some harsh,
And, among the latter (how it takes the breath!),
    planned emigration,
Alarm plucks at the heart of gentle Evangeline, knowing well
That first to go, for blacksmithing has come on evil days,
Must be her light of love, her hope, her heart, her Gabriel.

Gee, the paper's getting all wet!

Well, Gabe's unemployed, you see, so he comes squarely in the group the Gordon commission had in mind when it spoke of generous assistance (prison ships more likely) which would be given to those who would move to other parts of Canada to find jobs. And alas, it comes to pass that Gabriel is transported.

But Evangeline isn't the sort of girl who's going to take this expulsion bit lying down, and off she goes in search of Gabriel.

Suddenly, as if arrested by fear or a feeling or wonder,
Still she stood, with her colourless lips apart,
    while a shudder
Ran through her frame and, choked, the greetings died
    in her throat,
For there, pale and still, unmoving before her, was Gabriel,
And she beheld in a dream once more the home of her
    childhood,
Green Acadian meadows, with silver rivers among them,
Village and mountain and woodlands; and walking under
    their shadow,
As in the days of their youth, Gabriel rose in her vision;

But now he sat as she watched him inactive, unhearing,
    unheard;
Yet, he stirred as she dropped on her knees down beside him,
Kissed his quiet lips and laid his head on her bosom;
Sweet was the light in his eyes, but it suddenly sank
    into darkness
As when a lamp is blown out by a gust of wind at a casement.

Dead? Dead nothing.

When he was expelled from the Maritimes some influential Liberal friends had got Gabe appointed to the Senate.

Alice through the pipeline
or, the looking-glass revisited

HISTORICAL NOTE: For the most part, the Prime Minister sat silent through the long debate, leaving the direction of the Government's part to his Minister of Trade and Commerce.

"If only we had the most difficult part built for us we could finance this pipeline ourselves," said the murchison, "if only we had some help with the easiest part."

"It sounds like rather a lot of help," said Alice.

"Nonsense," said the murchison. "We are supplying most of the ownership in the company. The least you Canadians can do is supply the money."

Alice thought for a moment. "But if we put up the money," she said hesitantly, "shouldn't we be the owners then?"

"Nonsense," said the murchison again. "Greedy nonsense. You want everything, child? Share and share alike. If you will take care of the money when it is coming forward, we will take care of it when it is coming back. What could be fairer?"

"I can hardly believe it's fair at all," said Alice doubtfully.

"Can't you?" the murchison said in a mock-pitying tone. "Try again. Draw a long breath and shut your eyes."

Alice laughed. "There's no use trying," she said. "One can't believe impossible things."

"I daresay you haven't had much practice," said the murchison.

> Nothing pleases gas-men more
> Than taking frightful chances,
> They're of a type, on lines of pipe,
> To risk their whole finances.
>
> Or, rather, that's the story told,
> It strikes us here as funny;
> They're bright and brisk to take the risk
> —Except they'll use our money.

They were sitting side by side, each with an arm around the other's neck, and Alice knew which was which in a moment because one of them had DUM embroidered on his collar, and the other, CEEDEE.

38

"I suppose they've each got TWEEDLE round the back of the collar," she said to herself.

Tweedledum sat silent, stroking his moustache. He sat for a very long time, and although he was frequently asked to speak, he continued to stroke his moustache.

"A most peculiar way of giving leadership," thought Alice. "If I were leader, I think I would do more than that." She smiled suddenly. "Of course, I have no moustache. Perhaps that makes a difference."

"I hope you are not much tired," she said at last to the silent Tweedledum.

"Nohow. And thank you very much for asking," he said.

"So much obliged," added Tweedleceedee. "You like poetry?"

"Ye-es, pretty well—some poetry," said Alice doubtfully.

" 'The Pipeline and the Guillotine' is the longest," Tweedleceedee said, giving his brother an affectionate hug. He began at once:

> The House was told, "Provide at once
> This great financial prop,
> This loan of almost all the cost,
> With eighty million top."
>
> A member said "I really think. . . ."
> The guillotine went "Chop."

Here Alice ventured to interrupt. "If it is going to be all as horrid as that, I should prefer you would stop."

"It is going to be," said Tweedleceedee, "but who's to stop us?"

> Howe said, "I want this passed without
> A lot of raucous ruction,
> Each word you speak you know delays,
> A start upon construction."
>
> A member said, "I'd like to know. . . ."
> "You see?" said Howe. "Obstruction."
>
> The House was told it had to rush
> And dared not lose a day,
> "We've got," said Howe, "to get it built
> No matter what we pay. . . ."
>
> A member rose, Howe cut him down:
> "You've got too much to say."

"This is quite frightful," said Alice.

"You mean the story itself, or the verse?" asked Tweedleceedee, a note of menace in his voice.

"A little of both," said Alice, timidly, "if you don't mind."
"It's almost over," said Tweedleceedee. And he continued:

> "The time has gone," the axeman said,
> "To talk about this thing,
> To talk of gas and pipe and such,
> Of money on the wing
> Or whether Howe is in command
> Or murchison is king."

"Whatever became of Frank McMahon?" Alice asked after a pause.

"This chick has flipped," said Tweedleceedee.
Tweedledum said nothing. As usual.

Immigrants are mighty fine but it's you for me, ba-by

> "I don't believe any immigrant . . . no matter where he comes from, or how good he is . . . is as good as another Canadian baby."—*J. W. Pickersgill.* Mr. Pickersgill has since conceded that this was an observation he might better have left unobserved, but since it remains his only mistake, he has forgiven himself.

Ah, there. Here it is the jolly old, happy old day after Christmas. Back to the happy old Underwood. Yes, sir. And a merry old ho, ho, ho, to you too!

Boxing Day, so called because it is a day you frequently feel you'd be better off laid in a box, is with us once again. Yes, sir. A day for happy family gatherings, for jollity and games, a day for stomach powders.

In England, it's the day for the pantomine, those gay, colourful and tuneful presentations of strange and wonderful stories. Well we've got the raw material for some strange and wonderful stories right here in Ottawa. So prepare yourselves.

This is the story of a Cabinet minister, whom, for lack of a better name, we shall call Jack Pickersgill. (Actually, his name is Dick Whittington, but if you really throw yourself into the spirit of this

40

thing, you can believe it is what we just said.) When the story begins, the Hon. Mr. Pickersgill (or Whittington) is already in the Cabinet. In the past he has been a lecturer in history at the University of Manitoba, a civil servant, a trusted political adviser to a Prime Minister, all of which has fitted him to represent Newfoundland in the Cabinet and the rugged fisherfolk of Bonavista-Twillingate in the Commons. (Don't ask me why it fitted him for this; you've got to take some things on faith in pantomime.)

Anyway, to give himself something in common with his constituents, or to assume a sort of protective colouration, the Hon. Mr. Whittington (or Pickersgill) has just bought a schooner.

He sings a song tentatively titled, "He Was No Sailor When He Joined the Cabinet, but He's Been at Sea Ever Since." It goes like this:

When I was young and lived out West,
I swore the Prairie life was best,
Contented on my Western plain
I wished not for the bounding main
(The Main I knew was right at hand,
The after-end of Portage and . . .).

In thirty-seven, I came East,
As far as Ottawa at least,
And found in politics there lay
My true, my proper métier
(The motion of a rocking chair
Induced in me the mal-de-mer).

Earnest effort, long and hard,
Duly brought me high reward,
And I became the advocate
For Bonavista-Twillingate
(And still the sum I knew of fish,
Derived from seeing it on a dish).

And now to hold their love (and vote),
I've had to go and buy a boat,
With sailing jargon I'll be glib,
I'll batten mizzens, port the jib
(And yielding to the vote's compulsion
Dress like him on Scott's Emulsion).

The Hon. Mr. Pickersgill (or Whittington) goes off after dancing a sort of Red River hornpipe, which bears the same relationship to the real thing that a siscoe does to a Winnipeg goldeye.

41

In less time than it takes to say Jack Robinson (or Pickersgill) he is back again. It will be remembered that as Minister of Citizenship and Immigration, he made a speech in which he said that immigration is all very well, but it will never replace the cradle, or something like that. It was all a little confused. Now he explains, and there is a plaintive note in his voice as he sings:

Though preferring procreation by the native population
We resort to immigration to enhance our rate of growth;
Though I've otherwise been quoted, I should like to have it noted
That I'm really quite devoted to the products of them both.

My remarks were quite distorted when some journalist reported
That Canadians imported were a second choice at best,
What I said if they'd been heeding, was that those of
    native breeding
Were advantaged in not needing an adjustment to the rest.

That's the way I swear I said it, and no matter how you read it,
I would wish you'd do me credit by believing what I say,
I am shattered, I'm forlorn, at the thought the foreign born
Should detect a note of scorn and recall on voting day.

If there proves to be a demand for this song, sheet music will be marketed under the title, "I Meant What I Said When I Said It, but I Sure Got a Scare When I Read It." It should be suitable for singing at Girl Guide rallies, community gatherings, and campfire meetings of the Young Liberal Association. (Copyright reserved.)

In the finale—you'll realize we're skipping over a lot of this—in the finale, the Hon. Mr. Whittington (or Robinson) faces the electorate of Bonavista-Twillingate. He wears seaboots, a reefer coat over his middy blouse, and a yachting cap. He appeals to them as one of their own (to the extent, of course, that he appeals to them at all). He sings:

Yo-ho for the heaving deep lads,
Yo-ho for the briny blue,
Sing-ho for the wily cod, lads,
For the haddock and halibut, too;
The sea's in my blood and bones, lads,
I'm a seadog from Portage and Main,
Beware you, me hearties, of landlubber parties
—Return Skipper Jack once again.

That's all. Now if you will lie down and keep quiet, you'll feel better again in no time.

42

At least it's one problem that's no worry any more

Once upon a time, in a land far, far away there was a Finance Minister and he had a problem: his revenues gave him all sorts of latitude to make a tax cut, but he didn't know if it would be good for the country. (A year or so later this problem took wings like a bird and was never heard from again, but that's another story.)

In any case, there he was, nursing his fat-cheeked little conundrum. And there was Ko-Ko, who had got into the act in some inexplicable manner, singing:

> In his Treasury office, poor Harris he sat,
> Singing, "Money, much money, much money,"
> And I said to him, "Walter, pray what are you at,
> Singing money, much money, much money?
> Is it cuts in taxation you'd like to provide,
> But a fear of inflation won't let you decide?"
> With a pitiful sigh Walter Harris replied,
> "Oh, money, much money, much money."

(And where is poor Walter, now, pray?)

> He shed a salt tear as he thought of his plight,
> Singing, "Money, much money, much money,"
> For he wanted no voters to brand him as tight,
> With money, their money, much money;
> His advisers said, "Price-rise we've got to combat,
> And an increase of purchase-power hardly does that."
> He just moaned, "But my surplus is frightfully fat,
> With money, much money, much money."

Thus, as anyone well-versed in economics will recognize, he was faced with the to-be-or-not-to-be problem of fiscal policy-making—to be a schlemiel with the backbenchers or to be in wrong with the economists in the Finance Department.

> Then his backbenchers whispered, "Dear Walter do right,
> With money, much money, much money,
> If you cut voters' taxes our chances look bright,
> Oh money, much money, much money."
> Then he studied both sides and at length he said, "Yes,
> It is true that inflation may cause some distress,

43

But I'm not going to risk our bright hope of success,
For money, much money, much money."

Well, there you were, with the Finance Minister enmeshed in theories of cyclical—"cyclical," not "cynical"—budgeting, one of which, (the economists') holds that in good times you over-tax against a rainy day, and the other (the politicians') that it gets rainy just before an election.

And, now, leaving him to his problems, we come upon a pair of young voters. Their song:

> The voting that blooms in the spring,
> Tra la,
> One feels it is safe to surmise
> In the Budget some tax-aid will bring,
> Tra la,
> But that's an illusory thing,
> Tra la,
> In the next, why, your taxes will rise,
> And that's why we say you must catch on the wing
> The tax-cuts that fly in the voting-year spring,
> Tra la la la, tra la, tra la.

(The "tra la's" and the "tra la la la's" here, may be adjusted to the individual singer's needs, capabilities and perhaps even political inclinations.)

> The voting that blooms in the spring,
> Tra la,
> One feels will reflect in your tax,
> For the Minister's certain to wring,
> Tra la,
> From his Budget some pleasant small thing,
> Tra la,
> That's aimed to make voters relax.
> And that's what I mean when I say or I sing,
> Election year tax-cuts have always a string.
> Tra la la la, tra la, tra la.

And now shall we, just once more, join hands and recite the pledge of dedication to the Finance Department? "Every day, in every way, I am becoming a better and better taxpayer."

It *never came to pass, alas but, by George, it was different*

Until the late Conservative government hit upon the simple device of selling the stuff to hungry Communists, the most imaginative proposal for moving more of Canada's wheat belonged to the late James G. Gardiner.

There was never any public statement, but there were stories that the chesty little Minister of Agriculture had suggested informally to a couple of visiting British Cabinet ministers that a wheat-for-immigrants scheme might be arranged. It was never recorded how *they* took it, but Mr. Gardiner's Liberal colleagues were a little stunned. No wonder, for there were these questions:

If immigrants became an item of trade, where would they fit according to the General Agreement on Tariffs and Trade? Would British immigrants come in under the British preferential tariff? Or would there be any tariff at all?

> Said a Revenue man name McGee,
> "I wait with great interest to see,
> If we're to charge for 'em
> So much ad valorem
> Or if they'll come in duty-free."

And what of the immigrants who turned up at the dockside in Halifax unheralded? Since the purpose of the scheme would be equally to get rid of wheat and to bring in more people, care would have to be taken to see that payments were kept strictly in balance.

> Said the Government man at the pier,
> To an unannounced Briton, "I fear,
> That no shipment's gone through
> Swapping bushels for you
> —Would you mind simply eating them here?"

And would an even swap—a thousand bushels for one person was suggested—be fair in all cases? Should there, perhaps, be a special reduced rate (say five hundred bushels) for children under twelve years? Are Englishmen worth as many bushels (merely to state it is to show how ridiculous the suggestion is) as Scotsmen? Is the thin immigrant worth as much as the fat immigrant?

45

"If it's bushels for pounds we're exchanged,"
Said a woman, "it ought to be changed,
You should pay not alone
On my weight (just eight stone)
For it's frightfully nicely arranged."

Yes, and what of this?

A well-built young lady of Deal,
Said, "Really, I honestly feel,
For me, we should gain
Simply bags full of grain
Because of my great sacks-appeal."

Would all prospective immigrants be enthralled with the idea of their place at home being taken by a thousand bushels of Canada's best rust-resistant?

A hard-pressed young noble in Kent,
The last of whose fortune was spent,
Gasped, "Gad, sir, for wheat?
But a chap's got to eat."
So he took up the offer and went.

One can imagine the ancestral acres shortly thereafter blooming with No. 1 Northern. The family seat would have been saved because the Thirteenth Earl had made the sacrifice and migrated to Lemberg, Sask., or some other garden spot of the Dominion. It would be a story told and retold for generations in the family.

There was a young Scot of Dunblane,
Who looked on the scheme with disdain,
He said, "It's nae treat
Tae be bartered for wheat,
It goes, d'ye ken, 'gainst the grain."

And that's that the noo.

So there I was, glass in hand, taste buds at the ready . . .

If you drink nothing but water,
You'll never write anything wise,
But wine is the horse of Parnassus
That carries a bard to the skies.
—*Anon*
You said it, Anon.

—*Anon*

Sometimes it's almost a shame to take the money. The day, for instance, when the Commercial Counsellor of France on behalf of Les Membres du Comité des Vins de France, whoever they might be, held a wine-tasting, or réception-dégustation, as the invitation said. Herewith some fragmentary notes from the back of an envelope speckled with what may be Château Mouton Rothschild 1951 (a thoroughly bad year, by the way).

Invitation said 5:30 p.m. Arrive by cab at French embassy 5:30 p.m. Punctuality is a virtue. Struck again with thought that if a set-designer were given the job of creating what would represent a super-elegant embassy, he couldn't do much better than this. Acres of marble. Great sweeping staircase. Place dripping with crystal. Main reception room size of a football field, with ceiling-to-floor windows overlooking Ottawa River. One smaller room panelled in, of all things, birchbark. Crazy.

Time wasted reflecting on architecture: thirty seconds. Man at door handing out small parcels of literature, including book, *French Wines;* pamphlets entitled, *A French Art: How to Enjoy Wine;* programme for the evening stating, "In order to avoid mixing wines of different character, the tasting will proceed as follows—Wines A from 5:30 to 6:15, Wines B from 6:15 to 7:00, Wines C after 7 o'clock."

Arm self with glass suitable for Alsatian wine. Time 5:31. Late start.

Waiter heaves in view bearing two tall slender bottles—Gewurztraminer in one fist, Clos de l'Abbaye in other. Difficult choice, requiring thought running maybe to split second. Glass filled, encounter old friend who says, "What have you there?" Tell him Clos de l'Abbaye. He says, "How is it?" Tell him, great. He says, "I'm drinking Cha-

47

blis and I don't care for it." Tell him it goes well with oysters. He says, "I guess I should have brought an oyster." Peasant.

Glass no sooner empty than new waiter at elbow. Turns out to be an old-friend-type waiter who is serving at French embassy only for evening. Never heard of a free-lance sommelier before. Live and learn. Old friend has bottle of Chablis, bottle of Meursault. Lighten his burden by glassful of Chablis. Anxious to avoid suggestion of favouritism, later allow to have pressed on self small splashes of Meursault and Gewurztraminer. Feeling noble.

Meet old friend on French embassy staff. Discuss, at length, minute-and-half, problems of the day. No conclusions. Meanwhile tasting has proceeded to Wines B—red wines: Château Pontet-Canet 1952, Château Olivier La Garde 1947 (red Graves), Château Mouton Rothschild 1951, Pommard, Chambertin, Nuits St. Georges and Côte Rôtie. Bearing up bravely like a little man, distribute attentions fairly among them.

Run across old friend. Place filled with old friends, some of them brand new. Old friend introduces to French Commercial Counsellor. Speak to him of barbaric wine-marketing practices of Ontario Liquor Control Board. Diplomat to his shoelaces, he refuses to be drawn. Okay, it's his party.

Make way to buffet for bit of Brie on cracker—must keep one's strength up. Meet old friend going in other direction. Pleasant-looking man, friendly. Familiar but can't quite place him. Greet him, "How are you? Good party eh?" He asks if having good time. Tell him, absolutely. Exchange few words and go separate ways. Light dawns. French ambassador.

Press on regardless. Wines C now being served—Sauternes, Vouvray pétillant, Anjou Saumur Rosé pétillant; Champagnes: Taittinger Spécial Réserve Brut Blanc de Blancs (and a Blanc de Blanc to you, too) 1949, Moët and Chandon Dry Imperial 1949, Charles Heidsieck Brut 1949, Mumm Cordon Rouge and Pommery Sec. Must have popped enough corks to make a raft.

Meet old Deputy-Minister-type friend. Discuss whereabouts of Paul Martin. Strange subject.

Allow waiter to press on self glass of Vouvray. Dee-licious. Another old friend says, "Have you tried the Taittinger?" Admit not. Old friend smiles sublime smile. Obviously transported. Intercept waiter and examine his cargo; two other champagnes. Waste not, want not. Wast not, wante not.

Discover party much thinned out. Reporter, hard evening's work done, puts pencil on table, wine glass in breast pocket, and slopes off into night.

A wee peu de tolerance
or we'll claymore you, SVP

Note inscribed on a window-pane at the "Tam O'Shanter" by Burns* on reading a note in *Montreal Matin* declaring that Gaelic has no standing in Canada.

Tak' heed, *Matin,* you dwell among
Some millions wha frae Hielan's sprung,
Wha's weel-kent pride may well be stung
To do you battle;
You risk our wrath to slight our tongue
Wi' slandr'ous prattle.

The Gaelic's no' official here?
A foreign tongue? Calumnious jeer!
Tak' heed, *Matin,* to keep well clear
Of proud Cape Breton;
The chance you'd pass unharmed, I fear,
No Scot could bet on.

* Sam Burns.

49

Mr. Bones, what's your policy?
It's to get re-elected, Mr. Jones

> HISTORICAL NOTE: Since the general election of 1957, songs, dances and funny sayings—except, in the case of the last, those which occur by inadvertence—have not been prominent in campaigns. That year marked the high-water mark of music-hall influence in Canadian politics. Remember?

If he's going to avoid looking out of place, Louis S. St. Laurent may have to sing his speech, or accompany himself on the drum, when he appears at the big Liberal rally in Maple Leaf Gardens. The advance billing makes the whole show sound as if it could be moved over holus-bolus to the CNE Grandstand.

The *Toronto Daily Star,* which, with other outposts of the Liberal organization is handling ticket distribution, said in the caption under a layout of pictures the other day, ". . . plans have been laid to make it a real rootin'-tootin' affair with girls, bands, the Leslie Bell Singers, leading lights of the Liberal Party and a couple of surprise packages."

That's Uncle Louis in there, just behind the Leslie Bell Singers, and just ahead of the surprise packages.

> Oh, come to the rally! Oh, come to the fair!
> The Liberals are counting on thousands there,
> They're taking it easy on issues and facts,
> (Between all the speeches they've vaudeville acts)
> They find at this juncture it's prudent to dwell,
> On majorettes, dances and Leslie Bell.

Goodness knows what the surprise packages can be. Maybe the Prime Minister is going to disclose how he came to pick Paul Hellyer for the Cabinet. One theory is that Mr. Hellyer was picked because, being young, he helps to bring down the average age of an aging Cabinet. Or maybe it's because he can sing; the Prime Minister may have had the rally in mind all along. Anyway, it's got to have been something.

But, enough of this fruitless speculation; back to the St. Laurent show, a really big show, really big, and what the *Star* had to say about

50

it. As you know, next to Uncle Louis, the *Star* loves girls best, and of course a girl had to be got into the act. "Pert and perky Marianne Bauer, who will be much in evidence at the rally, wears Al Hollingworth buttons in her hair," said the *Star*.

The *Star* didn't mention pert and perky Mike Pearson, who will also be there (although possibly without Al Hollingworth buttons in his hair), or tall Paul Hellyer, or any of the Liberal candidates. But first things first.

> Oh, come to the meeting! Come to the fête!
> The St. Laurent minstrels are playing a date,
> The chief will exude his avuncular charm
> And Mike will recite, "How I keep you from harm."
> Between times it's whoops and a jolly hey-hey,
> With pipe-bands and singers and Cliff McKay.

That's Cliff McKay of TV's *Holiday Ranch*, who sings better than Mr. Hellyer and also plays a saxophone, but isn't a Cabinet minister. Injustice is everywhere.

The Liberals undoubtedly got the *Holiday Ranch* people into the rally to demonstrate how they're in touch with the farm population. A passel of TV farmers may be easier to be buddies with than the real thing, the Government's standing with the farmers being what it is these days.

The master of ceremonies for the Liberal soirée is going to be Lorne Greene, the man who sounds as if he were talking from the bottom of a rain barrel. When he was a humble news analyst, Mr. Greene used to be known as the Voice of Doom. It's something the Liberals might have given a thought to. He may carry a hex.

> Oh, join the assembly! Oh, fill the hall!
> The Liberals are planning on having a ball,
> They're not going heavy on talking sense
> (With questions and problems the acts dispense),
> No churl of a voter would dare complain
> At getting less Louis and more Lorraine.

That's Lorraine McAllister, who will also be taking part in the rally. She sings and, like Cliff McKay, isn't a Cabinet minister either. The other party referred to there is the one the *Star* listed on the programme between the Leslie Bell Singers and the surprise packages.

51

Doctor, I've got this pain, it's sort of, you know, like ow!

On two occasions it has been my misfortune (I suppose that pain *is* only a headache) to be closeted with a couple of thousand doctors assembled to tell one another how they go about things, like so many plumbers discussing the best ways to replace the trap in a drain or solder a leaky joint. There's nothing like a week in that sort of company (that's no ordinary headache; not like that, right behind the eyes) to set a fellow up. He's likely to go away worrying about ailments he never heard of striking him in places he didn't know he had.

Ever hear of Rift Valley fever? Oh, there's one for you. Sounds like something out of a Western, doesn't it, full of high mesas and cow-waddies and gringos?

> Git along, ol' pal,
> For there's no corral
> Once yuh hit that lonesome trail,
> An' yer pard, Ol' Paint,
> Got a dread complaint,
> An' no pinin' don't avail.
> Got that ol' Rift Valley fever,
> Got them symptoms plain to see,
> For yuh cain't mistake
> From the way ah shake,
> That it's round-up time fer me.

Yessir, that's what it is. Round-up time in the ol' Ward A.

Needless to say, a spell with doctors in convention assembled (I had a spell one day; came all over giddy) will have no effect on the steady, unimaginative, well-adjusted adult. It's a pity newspapers don't have more of them around so they wouldn't have to go sending hypochondriacs on that kind of assignment.

Ever hear of that old cough syncope syndrome? Kind of a melodious sounding name, ain't it?

> Got that ol' cough syncope syndrome,
> An' no more I'm gonna roam,
> Got that ol' cough syncope syndrome,
> Gonna flake out here at home.

52

When that coughin' fit comes git me,
An' my cheeks are turnin' black,
Gonna set an' never fret me,
Cause yo're here to pat my back.

Oh, those doctors, they're a million laughs. Get one up on his feet to explain how he's now bringing together incisions with Scotch tape and/or staples and the first thing you know he's got the old magic lantern going. If there's anything the lay reporter doesn't need at a medical convention it's coloured slides.

Especially before lunch.

Ever hear the etiological classification of something or other about pneumonia? Lovely. Sounds like a school yell. And epidural anaesthesia; that's got rather a lilt to it.

With epidural anaesthesia
Do they knock you out or freezia?

Pretty, that.

Then there was a doctor talking about psychotherapy who said: "I first encountered Dr. David Stafford-Clark on a bookshelf in a Saskatchewan bookstore many years ago . . . ." Well, of course, that brought Dr. Stafford-Clark back to everyone's mind. Agile fellow. Passion for climbing bookshelves. Once stayed so long the book dealer had to dispose of him at a remainders' sale. In Saskatoon that was.

Ever hear about the new viruses in humans that have been discovered since 1939 (a vintage year, with light delicate viruses that matured early and were notable mainly for their bouquet)? Among them were varicella and rubella.

Herewith a love song for two young viruses, a boy virus and a girl virus (orthodox, I admit, but nice).

Varicella, I whisper in wonder,
Varicella, my loved one, my own,
For I am your fella, my sweet Varicella,
And you are my virus alone;
Now why don't you wed your Rubella,
Together we're deadly as sin,
For once we join forces
The outcome, of course, is
The patient's as good as done in.

It's a catchy little thing, really. I see those two viruses going hand in hand down life's highway into the sunset (or into a patient, as the

53

case may be, not that it makes much difference to a pair of love-smitten viruses).

At one of their sessions, the doctors in question discussed how much the patient can be told about sickness and disease without unhinging him and starting him running up and down the walls. They didn't want to start up a lot of neuroses, they said.

Neuroses, for pity's sake? I've got a lot of oldroses here I haven't even touched yet.

Down in Greenwich Village
they wept when they heard

NEWS ITEM: Prime Minister, incapacitated by leg injury, summons Cabinet to bed-side meeting at official residence, 24 Sussex Street.

they ringed around in the fine old time-tuned house,
the bed whereon on flaccid sheets there lay
in pain, his ankle twisted, flat on his back
not unlike the national economy,
a gentleman, lately from the hustings come
and now, suffering not alone an astrolagus cracked
but a cabinet similarly incapacitated;
gone the multi-faceted dorion,
the hamilton whose post at posts now stands
yawningly vacant like so many more;
gone the docile browne, throttled in the joey clasp,
jacques flynn, and walker from his work at works,
and while the china-oriented west remains as his
tattered toronto must strike him less of his than hees'.

gone . . . but why add name on mournful missing name?
recumbent there, cocooned in clinging quilts,
his chest supports a burden not alone of loss
but also of state papers, problem-filled.
the cabinet, gap-mouthed and weakened though it is,
looks fit and well beside the state's accounts,
and thus in prelude those survivors there
bow, facing south, towards the i.m.f.;
and then to work, to prune, to cut and slash,

a promised causeway there, and here a raise,
a public building stopped before it starts;
how strange; how different when we chucked away our coyne
and now exist, not much on cash, but long on social credit.

they ringed around in the fine old time-tuned house
the four-poster, snowdrift-piled with problem papers,
holding beneath their very weight, still, unmoving,
not unlike the gross national product,
a gentleman lately from the hustings come,
soon to arise and go, not to innisfree but london,
there, there being no whoa to woe, to get more bad news;
pox on the inturned, upturned common market
upsetting trade patterns, denying preferences,
stealing bread from our mouths, our wheat from theirs,
fie on bright brave talk of atlantic bridges
when burning bright our own . . . and those behind;
and now the political tightrope, a test that no one begs
given, yet accounts in balance and *two* good legs.

Allan Ginsberg, move over. Man, like that swings, you know it?
Like I mean you can feel it, like heartbeats in the sands of time.

Got those diaper pail blues
gonna see them skits today

There turned up one day in a roundabout way—actually the stork
brought it—a copy of a letter received by a diplomat stationed in a
foreign land. It was from an official of the host government, and, after
the customary salutation, it read (Scout's honour) as follows:

"On the occasion of . . . Family Planning Day, we intend to have
some entertainment programme dealing with some aspects of family
planning.

"It will be a nice interchange of ideas if we depict our problems
on family planning as they exist in our respective countries in the
form of dance, drama, play, skit, silent acting, meno acting, etc. We
shall be grateful if you could participate and oblige."

Well, by George, that was a coincidence. It just happened that
there had been in course of preparation here a little folk-opera on

55

that very subject, available for next to nothing in case the Canadian government should have nothing on hand in the way of drama, skit or dance ("The Birth Control Cha-Cha"?) for the festival.

Our operetta, tentatively titled "Birth Control Without Tears," or, "Continence Apart," begins with the cast on stage singing, "We've Got Those Old Population Explosion Blues." It goes like this:

> To English wives in hairy tweeds,
> To soignée French and stolid Swedes,
> To Dutch on polders by the Zee,
> To mountain folk in Tennessee,
> To wives of Scotsmen dressed in kilts,
> To Siamese in homes on stilts,
> Alike to have-nots and to haves,
> To Bulgars, Turks, and Yugoslavs,
> To German fraus and zesty Danes,
> To intellects and feather-brains,
> To Arabs, Berbers, Balinese,
> To both the Red and Chiang Chinese,
> To Bedouin in goatskin tents,
> To film stars paying frightful rents,
> To Birchites and to Commie spies
> (A pregnancy's a grand disguise),
> To Zulu and to Hottentot,
> By plan, and very often not,
> Are daily born additions dear
> —It's getting mighty crowded here.

That's intended to impress upon the audience the universality of the problem. Obviously the host country has been worried about its population growth and it is our purpose here to give reassurance by pointing out that life is all around us, if I may coin that phrase.

At this point, to underline the individual aspect of the problem, we bring on a harassed-looking young woman who carries a feeding bottle in one hand, and swings a diaper pail from the other. Her song is "Nobody Knows the Trouble I Seen," or "I Ain't Got Rhythm." It goes:

> When I was still single and dreamt of the time,
> The time when at last I'd be wed,
> The future loomed rosy, the prospect sublime,
> Two hearts ever more would harmonically chime,
> What's happened since then's been a perishin' crime,
> —Oh, I wish that they'd shot me instead!

She wish-es they-ud shot her in-stead.

Five years from the wedding I'm bound to confess,
Confess I've a horrible dread,
If sensible shoes merely somewhat depress
I break out in spots in a helluva mess
At the sight of a baggy expandable dress
—Oh, I wish that they'd shot me instead!

CHORUS:
She wish-es they-ud shot her in-stead.

There's one little darling devouring the soap,
There's one who's just flooded his bed.
A third's got a fourth by the neck with a rope,
They say it's a wonder I manage to cope
(I couldn't except that I've taken to dope)
—Oh, I wish that they'd shot me instead!

CHORUS:
She wish-es they-ud shot her down dead.

Well, if there's a dry eye in the place after that, somebody around here is going to be surprised. It is therefore time for a change of pace, so we bring back the full cast of the Family Planning Players (every performance a sterile achievement) to sing something up-beat.

It will be enough here to sketch a couple of verses:

Rock, rock, rock,
Rock with Dr. Spock,
Give the kid a bottle, pat his little tum,
If he doesn't settle you could try a shot of rum;
Rock, rock, rock,
Rock at two o'clock,
That's the way you do it when you rock with Dr. Spock.

Rock, rock, rock,
Rock with Dr. Spock,
Hush him with a bottle, hush him as you can,
Remember for the future and plan, plan, plan;
Rock, rock, rock,
Rock around the clock,
That's the way you do it when you rock with Dr. Spock.

It's possible that a dance could be used here, if anybody really feels up to it.

57

It would be a good thing, too, introducing a welcome note of scholarship, to get in somewhere a number saluting the past great figures of the birth control movement.

Something might be built up around the theme, "I Cursed the Moment of Languor When I Forgot Margaret Sanger." Or:

> People's getting married late
> Had an earnest advocate
> In Robert Thomas Malthus who
> Said it was the thing to do,
> And also urged, as common sense,
> Subsequently, continence.

There is fertile (you should pardon the expression) ground in the life of Francis Place, a London tailor and labour leader, who decried the burden of large families on people of limited means. It would be interesting to know what Mrs. Place had to say on the matter, if she had time to say anything, what with having fifteen of Mr. Place's children to look after. Talk, talk, talk, that was Francis Place; but what did he ever do about it except write pamphlets?

Mrs. Place sings (this is just to give an idea):

> "I know," she said, "that you're sincere,
> I love you for it, dearie,
> But dammit, Frank, let's try this year
> Some practice with the theory."

That ought to send everybody home with something to think about, but goodness knows what.

Look, lady, protest is OK
but let's have some reserve

Oh, it may have been all very well in Canada to say it was just a case of Doukhobors being Doukhobors. But it was difficult to explain in Washington where people only know Douks as a form of the British nobility.

And how could anyone, even a Canadian, be sure at a distance whether it was simply a manifestation of Doukhobor exuberance and not the emergence of a new and distinctively Canadian form of political protest? Who was to say that another Minister of the Crown would not find himself similarly confronted because of some dissatisfaction with the tariff on plum jam? Might not an oilman's wife be found climbing on her chair at a meeting in Calgary South and divesting herself of her Dior to underline her demand for a more enlightened National Energy policy?

These were the questions one asked oneself as the newspapers blossomed with pictures of the Prime Minister standing exposed to some acres of bare Doukhobor pelt. Were we, in fact, faced with something like this:

"You've let us down," the woman cried,
"You're false," she said, "in word and deed."
The speaker heard; he must decide,
To answer her or pay no heed;

He chose the latter and went on,
He'd not so much as turned a hair;
Enraged, she shouted, "Out, begone,
Your views are more than one can bear!"
He heard again and even yet
Of ruffled feelings not a sign.
Her lips were clamped, her face was set,
Frustration etched its every line.
She said at last, "I'll make you learn,"
And then to show him how she felt,
She stood, and feigning unconcern,
She silently exposed her pelt.

"Great balls of fire," said the politician beneath his breath, "that woman has gone too far."

"I've been heckled with words and with gestures,
I've heard many things that were rude,
I've often been taunted and treated unwanted,
But none of those others was nude;
My hecklers have all had their clothes on
And, madam, I'd like to suggest
It's one thing to boo me, but please won't you do me
The honour of doing so dressed?"

One thing about it: that episode at Trail, B.C., when the Doukhobor women cast off all caution, among other things, in making their feelings known to John G. Diefenbaker, certainly had an elec-

59

tric effect on interest in the United States in the 1962 Canadian election.

In no time at all, nearly everybody knew that five naked women in Toronto, or one of those places, had paraded in front of the Prime Minister on the City Hall steps.

But enough of tedious fact.

> "Ah, ha," she cried, triumphant now,
> "You will not yield to words, of course,
> But like a politician bow,
> Before a show of naked force!"

> He blushed, and, turning to an aide,
> He muttered, "Will she never stop?
> Her protest's surely more than made,"
> (Beneath his breath) "go call a cop."
> The cop said, "Madam, be advised,
> While protest's always fair enough,
> There have been other means devised,
> Than stripping to one's very buff."
> They took her in, and as she went,
> She cried, "This crime's tomorrow's norm,
> And others soon shall make dissent,
> Sans hat, sans frock, sans Maidenform."

Is there a thought for an advertising campaign there: "I Dreamt I Went to a Political Meeting in My Maidenform Bra"? Or, "The Uplift Went Out of the Meeting When I Climbed on My Stool to Protest"?

Anyway, the harassed politician of our cautionary tale carried on:

> "I've been heckled and haunted and hounded,
> I've heard things both callous and crude,
> But still my composure's not up to exposures
> To women who heckle me nude.
> I suppose one could learn to endure it,
> But what makes the prospect so drear
> Is few at a meeting have even a fleeting
> Resemblance to Lili St. Cyr."

It may be that at a distance one worried too much. But it sounded alarming. Richard M. Nixon wrote a book about the six crises in his political life, and the worst of those was a debate in a kitchen with Nikita S. Khrushchev, who even had his hat on.

MILITARY

Principles of deterrence explained

I *dreamt I went to Alaska*
in my thermal maidenform shorts

Northway, Alaska

A guy could get bushed could get bushed could get bushed on a thing like this Exercise Sweetbriar. Thank goodness there's nothing wrong with me.

> The Northern Lights have seen strange sights
> But one no more they'll see,
> Five thousand men may come again
> —Among them won't be me.

For the past twelve frigid mornings I have risked becoming fast-frozen like a bunch of garden-fresh asparagus while pondering which mukluk is for the left foot and which for the right. A roving trapper now has informed me that, when the mukluks were handed out in Edmonton, I got two left ones.

> Turn up the steam and draw my bath,
> Lay out my finest clothes,
> These mukluks, parkas, Arctic vests,
> Are just for Eskimos.

Hamlets along the Alaska highway, all the gold now having been dug out of the ground, are directing their attention to digging it out of tourist pockets. Tourists would be well advised to see one of the world's few skin-covered brass doorknobs at No. 10 Wash House, RCE Maintenance Camp, Donjek River. That's where I grabbed a frosty doorknob at 30° below with a still damp palm.

> So a jolly old cheer for the Yukon,
> A mighty great whoop and hurrah,
> By day you go round in pyjamas
> And sleep out at night in the raw.
> (Rah, rah, rah.)

63

When the press party covering Sweetbriar were briefed for the ordeal at Edmonton, the members were told to wear the issue pyjamas by day instead of the issue longies because they are warmer. By night, said the briefing officers, shed the pyjamas because one sleeps warmer in a sleeping bag without them. It is significant that the army of about five thousand men slept not only in pyjamas but fully clothed most nights. They had thirty casualties evacuated, only a couple of them because of flu or colds. The press party numbering some thirty had four evacuated with flu and only two persons escaped either that or a severe cold.

> The heat and cold are both intense
> In tents;
> While sweating at the brow you freeze
> Below the knees.

If nothing else, Sweetbriar demonstrated to Northland newcomers the extremes of temperature that can be obtained in one small tent. The army tents, set on the cold, cold ground, were heated by small gas stoves. As any schoolchild knows (Hickenlooper's law) heat rises. Standing in a tent in the sub-Arctic it is possible to have something like a malarial fever up top and frostbite below. Only those who can stand on their hands can get warm all over.

> I'll never take these Northern Lights
> In place of gaudy neon,
> Nor any frosty northern trail
> For city streets with me on.

The Canadian Army issued Sweetbriar troops and observers with a high-quality sleeping bag in which it was possible to sleep like a log. The next thing is to get one in which you can sleep like a human. The fault of the sleeping bag was that it had two large sneaky zippers which in some sly manner moved around in the night until they were square in the middle of the occupant's back. Ever see a herring-bone-pattern spine except on a herring?

> Oh, give me a home where the taxicabs roam
> And it's not only minks that wear mink,
> Where 40° below is a thing you don't know
> And ice comes in cubes in a drink.

Exercise Sweetbriar is now over and it sure is a pleasure a pleasure a—there go those Northern Lights again—pleasure to be able to let you know I escaped getting bushed.

Sincerely,

GEORGE (Nanook of the North) BAIN

$\mathbf{T}$hose wedding bells are breaking up that old regiment of mine

Tucked away among my souvenirs with a small bundle of old dance programmes and my first corsage (which seems to have come back marked NSF—Not Sufficient Flower), there is an issue of the *Canadian Army Journal*.

That was the issue in which the editor departed to the extent of a couple of pages from the customary shop-talk about laying down enfilading fire and what Otter did wrong at Cut Knife Hill and allowed *Romance* to rear its head. Surprise? It was like striking oil in the backyard.

What he did was to reprint an article from the *British Army Review* of 1864—about love and marriage. Goodness only knows what got into him. The question the *British Army Review* was concerned with was "Should Officers Marry?" to which the answer implied was: "Only for the sake of the children."

In any case, one of its conclusions was that "extremes of heat and cold appear to be conducive to matrimony." In 1864, according to its reliable authority, there were two places where the young British officer stood in mortal danger of contracting matrimony—one of them India, and the other Canada. Of the two, the more dangerous was Canada.

Muffining and skating, that's what did it.

In eighteen hundred, sixty-four, about in Grandma's time,
A subaltern was posted to our frosty northern clime;
A single man and happy and to marriage not inclined,
Until our girls and winter sports conspired to change his mind.

The *British Army Review* said: "Setting aside the fact that in Canada . . . the girls are, as a rule, very pretty and tolerably well

65

educated, there is a delightful want of restraint about them that is positively charming. In England it might be put down as forwardness, but on the other side of the water it is regarded as spontaneous good humour . . . . They are generous, open-hearted, and hospitable. . . ."

> The girls he found were pretty, with a gay delightful air.
> He even found, surprised no doubt, their minds were passing fair,
> But what he mostly noted (one would judge without complaint),
> Was their open-hearted manner and their charming unrestraint.

Over to you, *British Army Review* of 1864: "Of all the peculiar institutions in Canada . . . sleighing and the skating rink must be characterized as the most delightful and, at the same time, most to be avoided. Flitting about here, there, and everywhere, in gaudy-coloured petticoats and the most bewitching of fur-tipped boots, the sirens glide . . . while distracted subalterns rush after them endeavouring in their madness not only to secure them as partners in the mazy dance of the rink, but in the mazy dance of life."

> In furry boots and petticoats designed to tantalize
> These visions skated to and fro before his dazzled eyes,
> His madness to secure one as his partner on the rink,
> Was such, I fear, he got involved much deeper than you'd think.*

We press on with the narrative: "The other great enjoyment throughout the winter is the sleighing; and surely no one will be rash enough to dispute the fact of its being conducive to matrimony. To the uninitiated, the phrase, "to muffin a young lady" may appear somewhat rude, but the simple meaning is that you are to offer not your heart but a seat in your sleigh to any lady you may choose to cavalier during the winter months."

> The downfall was completed on that second winter's day,
> That time he went to muffin with a lady in a sleigh,
> They skimmed along, so closely wrapped, in sundry skins
>   and furs,
> That when they disentangled, why, his heart was labelled "hers."

That's sweet.

Quote: ". . . the merry jingle of the sleigh bells is apt to make the nerves tingle, and the cosy warmth of the furs causes the heart to warm, and before the snow is off the ground it may possibly happen that 'your heart is no longer your own.' Marriages in North America

* On the other hand, maybe not.

66

amongst military men are of everyday occurrence, and the mess of
the regiment runs a very great risk of being altogether broken up."

> In eighteen hundred, sixty-eight, a family man by then,
> Our man, who's now a captain, gets a posting home again,
> And from the ship he looks his last upon those shores so fair,
> And angry, baffled curses rend the frosty northern air.

Quote: "Marrying men are most pernicious to a regiment."

Down, Pte. Engleby, down, and kindly stop licking my hand

Sometimes, in those quiet moments before sleep comes, a time I
usually give up to meditations on the bomb and the probability of
one's coming down with yaws, I spare a moment to wonder whatever
became of the beagles in the Canadian Army.

It was the *Canadian Army Journal* that brought us together, the
beagles and me. A captain who was stationed at Camp Borden—ah,
those distant, carefree days—wrote a piece which he was pleased to
title "Beagling as Training for War." It was an awakening, I can tell
you.

The captain was moved to put pen to paper, the *Journal* said, as
a consequence of his having been given the management of a pack of
beagles at the School of Infantry. (They can't have been drafted,
since we don't go in for that sort of thing. It hardly seems likely they
enlisted. To be quite candid, I don't know how the hell the beagles
came to be at the School of Infantry.) In any event, the captain
made quite a case for beagling. Hunting and soldiering have gone
hand in hand for centuries, he said, and he cited a number of for-
instances, including the following:

"Queen Boadicea encouraged her warriors to hunt before going
into battle, subsequently leading them to victory on the heels of their
successes in the hunting field."

Over the centuries there has come down to us a quatrain composed by one of the Queen's court which tells the story rather tersely
(but well):

67

> Fresh from hunting down the boar,
> Bo would lead her troops to war;
> This, plus frequent draughts of mead,
> Made her men quite brave indeed.

(Actually, it was the mead that did it. After they had been into that for a couple of hours they'd tackle wildcats. As a matter of fact, they frequently thought they *were* attacking wildcats. That mead will do it every time.)

It should be pointed out, in case it should lead to an investigation even at this late date, that the captain whose treatise on beagling is here under review, did whatever one does with beagles on his own and not on the Army's time. This he did notwithstanding the fact that many principles of war are also applicable to beagling, and presumably, vice versa. Or, as he said:

" . . . to follow the hounds with any degree of success demands the same qualities that are demanded of the present-day soldier."

> The private let moan in despair:
> "I wouldn't so very much care
> Being drilled like a hound
> If it weren't that I found
> That I'm really supposed to chase hare."

The captain went on to explain that lessons in camouflage, appreciation and description of terrain, and other subjects too numerous (I think the phrase goes) to mention, were to be learned from sniffing across the countryside with a pack of beagles.

"A few days with hounds will help develop in most followers who are prepared to take the trouble to learn," he said, "a useful eye for country and a healthy pair of lungs."

> *There's* a man with beagle training:
> Always tell it when you see
> How, although it isn't raining,
> He proceeds from tree to tree.
> —*Very old English countryman's verse*

Developing his theme, the captain said:

"The soldier who aspires to be an NCO (Nearly Collapsed Other-rank), or the NCO seeking a commission, can do no better in furtherance of this aim than spend his spare time following a pack of beagles at every opportunity available."

In other words, become an eager-beagle. Then:

Shed a tear for Private Smale,
There's a man who's going to fail,
Spends his time with army manuals,
And leans, in dogs, to cocker spanuals.

But, once more to our text: "Should he (the soldier) wish to make an even deeper study he would find several worthwhile examples of practical administration in the care, feeding and general maintenance of hounds."

(The nasty suspicion begins to raise its head here that what the captain is really trying to do is to unload that pack of beagles on somebody else.) However:

"Animal management is more closely related to man management than most people realize; the principles are almost identical, and failure to observe them is apparent for all the world to see."

Now *that* strikes a note.

The general care of dogs and men
Is more alike than many ken;
You will, I think, admit it's hard,
To tell some army food from Pard.

Y-o-o-o-o-o-o.

The voice of Bugle Ann?

No, the voice of Pte. Engleby. He just had breakfast. "Down, Engleby; down, dammit, down I say!" A can of sautéed Pard on fried bread in the morning and there's no holding him.

*A*nti / *not so anti-aircraft missiles I have / have not known*

Oh, there are going to be people who are not going to believe this— and, goodness knows, it is not mandatory—but back in the days of the Great Indecision, there was this little man and he . . . but let's take it as it was:

He came in, an unhappy-looking little man, and he said:

"It's a hard thing to say after all these years—how many is it, three?—but I'm still not clear about all this hoo-haw about these Bomarcs. Everybody keeps saying Canada's course is clear. Like that Mr. Justice Thorson was saying in Arborg, Manitoba (where, for Pete's sake, is Arborg, Manitoba?) like he was saying the other day, Canada's course is clear. He said like since the use of nuclear arms by Canada is not only valueless for defence, and unnecessary for deterrence, and also fraught with danger to the cause of peace, the course that Canada should follow is clear.

"Well, it ain't to me. Like, I mean, the argument should of taken place when the Government ordered the things, shouldn't it? What did everybody think they were going to put into them—geraniums?

"You could help me. Like if I could get a decent consensus I'd be willing to go along with that. The way it is, everybody seems to be saying something different, except the Government, which isn't saying anything."

Whereupon he put down a typed-up piece of paper and left. At the top of the form were the words "Strike out inappropriate words and phrases." This is what was underneath:

The Bomarc is a ground-to-air guided missile which [will/ will not/will with luck] knock down an enemy bomber at a distance [far enough/not nearly far enough] from the centres of population and industry [in Canada/the United States/both] to do [some/any] good.

The Bomarc [can/cannot] be fitted with nuclear and conventional high explosive warheads, both of which [are/are not] available. With a non-nuclear warhead, the weapon [can equally/ cannot within any stretch of the imagination] be effective against bombers which [are/are not] the mainstay of Soviet offensive power.

When it ordered the Bomarc missile and scrapped the programme for the [late lamented/unlamented] Avro Arrow, the Canadian government [decided "Yes"/decided "No"/hoped to heaven it somehow could avoid deciding at all] that nuclear warheads would be useful in warding off anything more troublesome than an infestation of snowy owls.

It is [wholly realistic/merely a product of Canadian self-consciousness (everybody is looking at us syndrome)] to say that if Canada is a non-nuclear power it will be a moral influence to help cause others to abandon nuclear tests [and/or] disarm totally. It is a fact that others [do/do not] give a tinker's hoot.

In any case, acquisition of nuclear warheads for the Bomarc [will/will not in any real sense] make Canada a nuclear power because warheads will be [wholly/partly/not at all] under the control of the Canadian government [if/when] they are obtained.

70

(In making their excisions, participants in this poll will seek to be consistent between at least the first part of the sentence and the end. This will be accepted as proof that they have no association with the Government in power.)

It is a matter which [ought to be taken into account/is wholly irrelevant and a palpable red herring] that Bomarc missiles which have a range of [300/400/500/0] miles [are only capable of being used against/wouldn't reach as far as] one foreign country—i.e., the United States. If the Government in a fit of warlike passion were to move these [devastating weapons/duds] to the farthest frontier, they still couldn't menace any land but Alaska, which is part of the United States.

The fact that Washington remains icily calm in the face of this danger indicates that Washington [does not believe Canadian malevolence goes that deep/knows it is going to keep strings on the warheads so that they can be used only in the event of an attack by a third party/is not convinced the Bomarcs can do much harm to anything anyway]. (Choice limited to two.)

So far as third parties are concerned, it is [pertinent/impertinent] to observe that should they choose the role of burglars they aren't entitled to complain about what the householder keeps to [shoot them/shoot *at* them] with.

The Canadian government will make its decision [soon/after an election/never if it can help it].

Footnote: As to the operational performance and probable worth of the Bomarc, the quiz, of course, remains valid today. As to the last question, the answer turned out to be (3).

Blenheim, Oudenarde, Waterloo, Lucknow, and Buckingham Palace

Cor, they've gorn an' done it.

> They're changing guard at Buckingham Palace,
> Christopher Robin went down with Alice,
> The Guards were on duty behind the fence,
> "It doesn't look grand, but it does make sense," says Alice.

Monday morning there they were, all dressed up, parading up

and down behind that ruddy great fence. Proper lot of Charlies they looked. And there were the tourists, peering through the bars, like people at a zoo.

> They're changing guard at Buckingham Palace,
> Christopher Robin went down with Alice,
> Now they don't trip over visitors' feet,
> "A guard on his face is far from neat," says Alice.

All during the summer, even when the disquieting battle reports were coming in—reports of rearguard actions being fought against superior forces of tourists—hope remained alive that the Guards would hold and fight back. Thin red line of 'eroes and all that.

For a moment there, when one of the Guards fetched a woman from Boise, or somewhere, a sharp clout on the shin with his rifle butt, it looked as if they might win.

> They're changing guard at Buckingham Palace,
> Christopher Robin went down with Alice,
> Descendants of men of the British square,
> "But tourists is more than a man can bear," says Alice.

The Guards, as a battlefield communiqué might put it, had to retire in the end to previously prepared positions—inside the Buck House fence.

Now—change, change, change; is nothing sacred any more?—there is talk of the Horse Guards changing from changing guard in the courtyard where they've changed guard for two hundred years to changing guard in Horse Guards Parade.

I'm not sure what the effect of that will be—I'm not even entirely sure I understand what I've written—but I'm prepared to be alarmed. Horses aren't any bigger than they were two hundred years ago, heh? Why, then, has the courtyard become pokey all of a sudden, heh? If a Labour government had been in, a man would have known where to look for the culprit; India all over again.

Meanwhile, back at the Palace . . .

> They're changing guard at Buckingham Palace,
> Christopher Robin went down with Alice,
> Fearless the Guards facing shot and shell,
> "In summer the Palace is living hell," says Alice.

It is to be hoped the authorities have thought out the possible consequences of this moving of the Guards behind the fence. What, for instance, if camera-laden tourists in their frustration start setting upon off-duty Guardsmen as they stroll from Wellington Barracks in mufti?

What then, heh?

Goodness knows, an off-duty Guards officer in his tight-trousered dark suit, carrying a tightly-furled umbrella, with his curly-brimmed bowler resting on the bridge of his nose, is quite as picturesque a bit of Olde England as any guardsman in a scarlet tunic, blue pants and a bearskin head-muff.

> They're changing guard at Buckingham Palace,
> Christopher Robin went down with Alice.
> A Guard stood exposed in his sentry box,
> "They're fitting them soon with doors and locks," says Alice.

And what about that guard that is sent out each night to guard the Bank of England? This guard of fifteen men marches—yes marches, on foot—right through the crowded streets, from Wellington Barracks to the Bank down in the City. At rush-hour. And with no protection from the traffic but a hurricane lantern which the end man swings like the trainman in the caboose of a freight.

They've been at this nightly lark since 1780, but if some of 'em get to finking about 'ow their mates at the Palace are being pertected from the wicked tourists, first thing you know they'll be wanting to go by ruddy cab.

> They're changing guard at Buckingham Palace,
> Christopher Robin went down with Alice,
> "The next thing you'll see is a printed card
> Saying, 'Visitors Kindly Don't Feed the Guard,'"
>   says Alice.

They're changing guard at Buckingham Palace. Christopher Bain went down with his mother. He said, "Chicken!"

The day they closed the door on a cellarful of memories

Denman Street is a crummy little street in the very beginnings of Soho, a stone's throw away from Piccadilly Circus, or about as far away from the celebrated roundabout as a man on leave could throw his pay, which he frequently did. The street had at least four clubs—allowing for the unlikely event that I missed one—three of them in cellars and one in a loft. None of them was ever in danger of finding itself listed among London's better clubs, social, political, military, night, or any other kind. But they had large and devoted memberships—the devotion to any particular one rising and falling according to the state of its beer supplies—and among the members were many Canadians; very many Canadians.

To identify the clubs: there was the "Tudor" where the custodian, Peggy by name, was blown down the entrance steps into the club premises the day the buzz bomb hit the Regent Palace Hotel; the "Crackers," where a Canadian once bit the proprietress's dog in pursuit of some forgotten research; and the "Jacobite," where one member was known sometimes in moments of exhilaration to leave by the drainpipe rather than risk himself to the stairs.

The Fourth, which this is about, was the "Chez Moi," a place that once just after the war, got itself described in the *Daily Mirror* as "a cellarful of gallantry." It was the only one which hadn't closed or changed hands.

"It's not really a cellar," the *Mirror* went on to say." It's a long underground room with a long bar, a few saddleback chairs, a big fireplace—and atmosphere. Plenty of atmosphere. And, of course, an out-of-tune piano.

"The name is the 'Chez Moi Club' in Soho and every air ace of this war who has come to London and who is not a rabid teetotaller has climbed down its unlit stairs at one time or another."

Archie Lewis, who was the custodian of that out-of-tune piano from 1938 until mid-1942, and who returned again in the mid-1950's, got to reminiscing about it one day. The piano had a metal top, he recalled, to keep the beer from dripping into it. Not that that did much to save the piano's inner workings, for some of the customers were in the habit of lifting the lid and pouring the beer in, sometimes without taking it out of the glass.

Archie recalled, too, that the customers frequently were hospitable to the piano player, which did the piano player's piano playing very little good. One night when it had brought his piano playing to a dead stop, the proprietor, Harry France, said that if Archie wasn't going to play, he might as well go home. Wounded, as any artist would be, Archie slammed down the keyboard lid—on the fingers of his other hand.

Mickey Cronin was on the door of the "Chez Moi" during the

war. His hours were nominally from three in the afternoon to eleven at night, but in practice they might be from three to eleven, or to six, or to half past three, or whenever before eleven the beer ran out.

During the blitz, proprietor and staff sometimes used to sleep in the club, which had the double advantage of keeping them close to their work, and saving them the wear and tear of running to and from bomb shelters, the club being in a basement anyway.

One night a bomb brought a large piece of concrete crashing down on to doorman Mickey Cronin's bed—a large enough piece of concrete to carry the bed into a sub-basement. Fortunately, the doorman had left it a short time before to investigate another noise elsewhere.

Harry France took over the "Chez Moi" just before the war. During the war, he operated what amounted to a branch bank. He used to cash about £1,000 a week in cheques, and in six years of war he lost only £60. He probably made a bit of money, too. He ran the club for more than a score of years and in that time he met crowds of people, collected dozens of pictures of people in and out of uniform, and gathered a clutter of trophies, including a picture of himself framed in a toilet seat—a Canadian gift.

There were pictures of Canadians and Canadian pennants on his walls, and lots of Canadian names in his membership lists. For a long time after the war, he continued to hear occasionally, by phone, from a Canadian in Moncton who would ask how the club was going, but who never came back. Also, from time to time, the place continued to be awash with Canadians—RCAF people on leave from the Continent, or on stop-overs on ferry flights to and from Canada and Europe.

When one day, after a very long time, I heard that the club was going to be closed and the building turned over to the wreckers, I went around to have a look. That cellar had seen gong parties, and wakes and commissioning parties, and end-of-tour parties, and parties without any excuse. Nothing had changed, except that the place was no longer jammed to the doors, blue with smoke, and rocking with noise.

A few days later, Harry France shut the door and prepared to move away from the crummy little street to a new club in the pleasant southwest town of Poole, in Dorset. He said as he went that all memberships were being transferred—but, of course, you can't transfer a memory.

Ye olde independente deterrent she ain't what she used to be

In other days, Harold Macmillan's trip to the Bahamas to win something from John F. Kennedy to replace the Skybolt missile, would have been recorded in song for the ages.

However, nobody has been writing any new Olde English drinking songs lately (which are songs of the sort that events of that sort ought to be drowned in). So, for the benefit of those who have grown tired of wassailing and otherwise carrying on with Olde English drinking songs, herewith a new Olde English drinking song.

It is called, "I Met My True Love Under the Mistletoe in Nassau" (it will be remembered it was a Christmas meeting), or, "I Got the Missile but I Think I Also Got a Bit of the Toe."

> Sing, ho, merry, merry,
> Fa diddle, fa la,
> Macmillan's come back from the West, ho;
> He went out to Nassau to parley with Jack,
> They made an agreement on means of attack
> (They're talking in Britain of shipping him back).
> Sing, ho, merry, merry,
> Fa diddle, fa la,
> Macmillan's come back from the West, ho.

(Everyone at this point beats his pewter mug on the table and chants, "The independent nuclear deterrent forever.")

> Sing, ho, merry, merry,
> Fa diddle, fa la,
> Macmillan's come back from the West, ho;
> He gave up the Skybolt for cost and delay,
> Its failures in tests were a source of dismay
> (They fired one on target the very next day).
> Sing, ho, merry, merry,
> Fa diddle, fa la,
> Macmillan's come back from the West, ho.

(It is said that the British Minister of Defence, Peter Thorneycroft, wanted to get U.S. Defense Secretary Robert S. McNamara around the wassail bowl. He was going to give him his Christmas punch.)

> Sing, ho, merry, merry,
> Fa diddle, fa la,
> Macmillan's come back from the West, ho;
> He's brought him a missile to fire from the sea,
> From under the waves, where, as all will agree,
> It's quite dicey business for bombers to be.
> Sing, ho, merry, merry,
> Fa diddle, fa la,
> Macmillan's come back from the West, ho.

("I say," said the Air Marshal, "our blawsted deterrent is based on the V-bomber force and old Mac's brought back with him Polarises, which are fired from submarines. Odd chap, heh?")

> Sing, ho, merry, merry,
> Fa diddle, fa la,
> Macmillan's come back from the West, ho;
> A pilot said, "Really, I'd give it a bash,
> It's not as you know that I'm fearful I'd crash,
> But water plays hob with my air force moustache."
> Sing, ho, merry, merry,
> Fa diddle, fa la,
> Macmillan's come back from the West, ho.

(Actually, all these "sing, ho, merry merries" don't mean anything, and are only thrown in to give the thing some faint flavour of authenticity. However, if the wassailing goes on long enough, nobody's going to care.)

> Sing, ho, merry, merry,
> Fa diddle, fa la,
> Macmillan's come back from the West, ho;
> A young naval person, with hanky in sleeve
> Groaned, "Really, one finds it quite hard to believe,
> From Nelson to NATO—my God, how I grieve."
> Sing, ho, merry, merry,
> Fa diddle, fa la,
> Macmillan's come back from the West, ho.

77

Steady there, Nikita, steady, can't you see we're snowbound?

If Nikita Khrushchev's spies are on their toes, one of these wintry days the jig could be up. Once they get word back to the Kremlin about what happens in Washington after a heavy snowstorm, there goes the old ballgame, preparedness-wise.

What happens in Washington after a heavy snowstorm is Nothing. Things stop.

> If the Russians should attack us, they'd be well
> advised to know,
> We should think it most unsporting if they did it
> after snow.
> We've got many mighty missiles and a plenitude of
> planes,
> But we're lacking in equipment to unplug our traffic
> lanes;
> Thus on mornings after snowfalls it's a fact one must
> relate
> That the Pentagon stands darkened and that all is
> shut at the State,
> Then the button stands untended, then their chance is
> quite unique
> Then a sudden strike would find us well and truly up
> the creek.*

(All right, so it's not T. S. Eliot; so look to him for warning when the time comes.)

One morning of indelible memory, Washington was what sometimes goes by the name of a regular fairyland. In other words, it was eight inches deep in snow. The day before, after it had been snowing all day, it was announced that Plan One would be put into effect. Then, if things got really desperate, Plan Four. In the end, what they came up with was what I think was Plan Eleven. That apparently stated that everybody was supposed to stay home and huddle by the fire. From all available evidence "everybody" included the snow-plough crews, if any.

* Without a paddle.

When daybreak showed the city in the grip of winter lay,
Administration sources ruled a shutdown for the day,
And agencies which still pressed on were thinly staffed
    and few
(A tiny band at CIA looked south to plot a coup),
And who could help but wonder, with a soupçon just of
    dread,
Was the finger of deterrence on some shovel-shaft instead?
But while Washington surrendered, barely functioning at most,
Undaunted by the weather, Dauntless Bain was at his post.*

What is needed here is a demonstration of the sort of interdependence that everyone keeps prating about. Plainly, Washington hasn't got enough snowploughs. Ottawa, on the other hand, hasn't got enough air conditioners. (That, of course, is a totally unrelated matter and has nothing whatsoever to do with the question before us at the moment, which is how to keep Washington functioning in winter.)

Where were we? Interdependence. Snowploughs. Does it begin to come clear? What is needed is a North American Snow Defense Command—Blades across the border! Any snowdrift of yours is a snowdrift of ours! When it's coldest our friendship is warmest; and all that sort of thing.

I see the red-faced men of this force in toques with tassels, flannel undervests and wool shirts, knee boots, and, when decorated for gallantry (for energetic snow-shovelling beyond and above the call of duty), wearing the ribbon of the golden truss, with crossed palms, anguished.

Anyway.

If the forces of our nations are to give each other aid,
There's a field where further study ought no longer
    be delayed;
If the military planners had a meditative browse,
Could they not devise some sort of scheme, like NORAD,
    but for ploughs?
With weather-warning radar and an airlift to give speed,
The ploughs of both could be combined to serve the
    common need;
Given decent forward planning, there's no reason not to have
The Elgin Street equipment clearing Pennsylvania Ave.

* Thinking, thinking, thinking.

There.

I don't look for much from a couple of grateful governments.
It does give me a little twinge, however, to think that we gave up
knighthoods.

Off we go into the wild blue (white supremacist) yonder

NEWS ITEM: The Confederate Air Force is trying to
obtain a World War II Japanese Zero to add to its
collection of World War II aircraft. The Confederate
Air Force is dedicated to "the preservation of the
world's fighting aircraft, and pledged to support and
promote the customs and traditions of the Deep
South."

The light is quickly fading o'er some secret southern base,
And a sense of deep disquiet quite enshrouds that solemn place,
For the planes are in the hangar, but for one that's airborne still,
It's the ship of Captain Ashley, or the Cornpone Escadrille.

Conversation:
A. He oughn't to of gone up there in a crate like that. It war'
nothin' but suicide.
B. Captain Ashley is a brave man, and a gentleman; a Southern
gentleman.
A. Anybody who ever saw him heave a brick at a federal marshal couldn't doubt that none.

But hark there, don't you hear it; don't you hear that distant sound?
Captain Ashley's coming, limping—can he make it to the ground?
And he does, and sits there slumping, tense and white about the mouth,
And you know he's fought his heart out for the customs of the South.

It fair tears yer heart out, don't it?

For his Daddy had a lynch-rope, and *his* Daddy cracked a whip,
And the Captain's never been inclined to let such customs slip.
He does honour to his forbears, does this dedicated ace,
As he heeds their admonition—"Keep the Nigra in his place!"

So he flies his dicey missions, unescorted as a rule,
As he terrorizes children in some integrated school,
Or he frightens would-be voters who've the nerve to think they rate
Just a touch of equal treatment in a democratic state.

The South Shall Rise Again. Up the Confederate Air Force.

Turn in your bomb, Fogarty, you've couped your last coup

> There is a bill in Congress described as the Central
> Intelligence Agency Retirement Act of 1964 for
> Certain Employees. The Certain Employees are spies.

It is the sort of thing to which the ordinary person probably never gives a thought, but Congress, humane to a fault, does think about it. What happens to old spies when the times comes, as it must to all men, when there is no longer any zest for the day's coup?

Give a thought for the spy who's not youthful,
Whose cravings for action depart,
Who, plotting a coup, knows just what he must do
But finds he's reluctant to start.

It makes a fairly heart-rending thought. There's James Bond, or at least his equivalent in the CIA, his trenchcoat now inadequately hiding the bulge at his waist, crouched behind a palmetto bush and reluctant to leave it to go out and egg on the revolutionaries.

His hat can't quite hide his bifocals,
(A hairpiece resides underneath)
And now he escapes from his various scrapes
By the skin of detachable teeth.

Meanwhile, back at the hotel, a lissom girl waits, disenchanted. Some spy. Last night at Rick's—ahh, Rick's in the old days; things had been different then—she had overheard his whispered instructions to the bartender: "An eight-to-one martini, José; one part gin, eight parts Geritol."

81

His Beretta tucked into his girdle,
A knife in elasticized hose,
He tracks down his clues (in his arch-support shoes),
As he matches tired wits with his foes.

"It's the end of the road, Fogarty; you're all washed up. There's no room for tired spies in the CIA." It had come to that. The old head bows. After all these years, after all those crummy places— Guatemala, South Vietnam, Cuba, the back-alleys of half the world —all washed up.

"Sorry, too old."

"Sorry, we're not hiring any spies today."

"Leave your number and if anything comes up, we'll call you. Don't call us; we'll call you."

Shed a tear for the agent who's aged,
Who finds that the grind casts a pall,
Whose greatest delight when he's off for the night
Is to sit by the fire in his shawl.

Well, it was all done now.

The place is a sleazy waterfront bar somewhere in the sub-tropics.

"Who ees the Gringo who seet all day weeth the cheap booze?"

"You don' know? That ees Señor Fogarty. He was beeg spy wance with CIA. Now he jos seet there saying 'Shilling a day, blooming good pay; lucky to touch it, a shilling a day.' "

"That ees Kipling, no?"

"No, I theenk eet ees call' poverty."

How poignant; this spy, once a master,
Once nerveless when danger was rife,
Now weakened and strained and all varicose-veined
And cast off in the sunset of life.

But wait! What is this item in the newspaper?

Congress has before it House Resolution 8427 "to provide for the establishment and maintenance of a Central Intelligence Agency retirement and disability system for a limited number of employees."

By George, Congress may make it possible for him to raise his head again yet! Maybe it is still not too late even—dare he hope?— to find Margaret again; Margaret and the kids. But that was a lot of drinks and girls ago.

82

Let us pause to remember the agent
Whose talents by age are impaired,
Just think, at his peak what a consummate sneak
—Let him know by his pension you cared.

But what's this letter from an anonymous CIA man that Congressman Allen Smith of California has read into the Congressional Record?

"Already employees in their thirties are making plans to get advanced degrees by going to night school, thereby lessening the effectiveness of their daily work, in order to get a better position outside when their fiftieth birthday comes around."

His lip curls in a faint sneer. The old shop must be a changed place. Night school? In his day spies knew what the nights were for.

With a barely perceptible nod he commands a fresh drink. To hell with Margaret and the kids. Once a spy, always a spy.

A loaf of bread, a jug of wine, a Polaris and thou, Admiral

It's no secret that the Admiralty in London is unenthusiastic about that allied fleet of freighters that would be sent out with mixed crews to sail the world's seas with Polaris missiles in their holds.

Now it turns out that one of the reasons is the administrative difficulty that would be presented by the different policies on drink. Rear Admiral G. T. S. Gray, senior naval member of the directing staff of the Imperial Defence College, has noted in an article in the (U.S.) *Naval Review:*

"British sailors by tradition are entitled to a daily rum ration; French are not. French sailors receive a daily allowance of wine; Germans do not. German sailors are allowed to purchase schnapps and whisky in their ships; Italians are not . . . ."

Admiral Gray suggests no solution exists which would not result in an unhappy, disgruntled and inefficient ship.

Fortunately it happens that a solution *does* exist which conceivably could result in an inefficient ship—but an unhappy one, never. In fact, it could be counted upon to produce as gruntled a lot of sailors as has ever been known in the long history of seafaring.

83

Obviously the thing to do is to combine the practices of the several navies from which the sailors would be drawn.

> Give me a berth in a missile ship, and a place in a
> NATO crew,
> Where customs tend to become a blend of what
> several nations do,
> So the tot of rum and the glass of schnapps,
> with the wines of France contend
> And our favourite port is the vintage sort—we've a pipe
> of the '22.
>
> CHORUS:
> "Have you missiles down below, Billy Boy, Billy Boy,
> Have you missiles down below, charming Billy?"
> "Yes, we've missiles down below
> But they're full of rum, you know,
> We're a fun ship and not like any other."

Does this idea begin to shine in all its luminous brilliance, Admiral? An unhappy ship, indeed! Why, the boatswain will have to stand with a bat at the top of the stair (gangway? ladder?) to keep people from joining unbidden.

Bent on making some obscure point of objection, Admiral Gray says: "By other people's standards, Norwegian sailors eat a lot of fish." It is hard to say what sort of problem this is supposed to present; with the right wine, a Sole Walewska is a proper treat. Any Italian, British, French or German sailor would be a clod who failed to appreciate it.

> Give me the heave of the spume-swept deck, and the song of
> the soughing sea,
> Give me some chaps who are filled with schnapps, who will
> serve by the side of me;
> We're a mixed-in lot in the NATO fleet, and our purpose is
> dim perhaps
> But we know that fish is a better dish for a bottle of good
> Chablis.
>
> CHORUS:
> "Aren't your missiles then a spoof, Billy Boy, Billy Boy,
> Aren't your missiles then a spoof, charming Billy?"
> "No, they're not a sort of spoof,
> They're all eighty over proof,
> We're a fun ship and not like any other."

"Is it a feasible proposition," Admiral Gray asks, "to consider, for example, Belgian, Norwegian and Italian sailors working under a French commanding officer whose only foreign language ability is English?"

Frankly, yes it is. In a happy ship, a few simple phrases will suffice, such as, "Pass the port." The use of this phrase on the bridge could conceivably lead to confusion which would cause the ship to be steered endlessly in left-hand circles. However, confined to use at table, no such difficulty would occur. And if it does, is anyone going to care, really, deep, deep down?

> Give me the sting of the flying salt, and the lash of the
>   seaborne gale,
> Give me my tot in a copper pot, for a womanly drink
>   is ale;
> But the Meursault at lunch was rather good, and at dinner
>   last night I thought
> That the Haut Brion (which is almost gone) went frightfully
>   well with quail.
>
> CHORUS:
> "Can you make those missiles fly, Billy Boy, Billy Boy,
> Can you make those missiles fly, charming Billy?"
> "Yes, we'll make those missiles fly
> If we're steady by and by,
> We're a fun ship and not like any other."

Certainly, it doesn't smack of the Nelson tradition to find an admiral of the Royal Navy throwing quibbles in the way of what promises to be one of the great naval experiments since the owl and the pussycat went to sea.

This, for instance, is a quibble: "British sailors are allowed all-night leave; German sailors must be aboard by 2300 hours."

Obviously, there are two solutions to this problem. Either the Germans can be allowed all-night leave, or the British must be allowed to bring their girls to their quarters. (Students at Harvard have been doing it, and no Jolly Jack Tar could complain if he . . . . Well, there *were* allegations of . . . what shall we say? Revels?)

Since the Italians do not seem to have contributed anything to the drink arrangements, and having Sophia Loren and company in mind, perhaps the Italians as a contribution to the general camaraderie could make their datebooks available.

85

Give me the cry of the haunted gull, in the place where
    the north wind skirls,
And a man commits all his strength and wits as the NATO
    flag unfurls,
And our ways with drink will be all our ways, and our ways
    will leave the Brits',
And we'll integrate at a famous rate—the Italians will bring
    the girls.

CHORUS:
"Can you fire them over there, Billy Boy, Billy Boy,
Can you fire them over there, charming Billy?"
"Yes, we'll fire them over there,
If we're not too looped to care,
We're a fun ship and not like any o-o-th-er."

No wonder NATO is in trouble. No imagination.

LONDON

The natives have strange ways

I *dreamt I dwelt in marble halls (with CHW, CH and a WC)*

Once upon a time, which is the way all such stories should begin, some people went to London to live, and in no time at all they could talk knowledgeably about c and c, and f and f, chw, ch, and ono, not to mention separate wc with low flush suite. (A low flush suite is one with a handle and differs from the other, which presumably is a high flush, like a king high in poker, in that the other has a chain on which one chins oneself to release a cataract resembling the Zambesi falls.)

Enough. English plumbing is too terrible a subject to dwell upon.

Anyway, there were these people who went to England and were househunting. They combed the ads and they listened to the friends who said, "The only place, the *only* place to live, is in the country," and the other friends who said, "You'll die in the country, simply *die*." From the ads they learned that c and c means "carpets and curtains," f and f means "fittings and fixtures," and chw means "constant hot water," which means that the landlord is lying in his teeth.

The first thing they knew, the only thing that was on their minds was plumbing. ("Yes, doctor, it was in about September that I started to get this fixation about plumbing. I don't know; it just seemed that I started seeing pipes everywhere, running up the outside walls, running down the inside walls, never decently interred *in* the walls.")

Where were we? Oh, yes; terminology. Well ch stands for "central" and "heat"—"central" meaning that wherever the radiator is, that's the centre, and "heat" meaning that if a wet finger won't actually stick to the pipes, that's it. The people we are writing about found one place which the owner, in a flight of delirious fancy, described as having electric central heating. Electric central heating! Six rooms, each one with an electric grate in it. Guaranteed to keep you warm running down to the bank to make payments on the overdraft.

89

(You know, about plumbing—there's reason to believe that Englishmen don't really trust plumbing. Not deep, deep down in their hearts. If they can't actually see it and hear it, they don't believe it's earning its keep. They like it to be where they can keep an eye on it, as in the house where a disposal pipe, six inches in diameter, sturdy as an oak, rose majestically from the living room floor and disappeared just as majestically through the living room ceiling. Close to the wall, mind you, but not in it.)

But we digress. Terminology. ONO means "or near offer." ONO, like the shrunken head on the mantlepiece which was all that was left of Uncle Willie after the Indians got him, is just a conversation starter. The chap who doesn't advertise ONO doesn't expect to get his price either. He's just waiting for the other chap to speak first.

(Do you know what a "lagged tank" is? A lagged tank is a tank in the attic with a jacket around it to keep it from freezing. The people who are going to use the water from it if it doesn't freeze, which it probably will anyway, aren't going to have their jackets and mittens on when they wash. But the water tank will be comfortable.)

Well, the people we are writing about finally found a house. To rent. That is, to buy and to rent. That is, to buy the C and C and F and F (see above and good luck to your reason), and to rent the premises with an additional charge for the CHW and the CH (see above again).

Having found it, these people moved in—but only after a lot of palaver with a firm of solicitors which had an Old Public Schoolboy's *Who's Who* (Eton) in the waiting room, and a lot of presumable Old Who's Who (Eton) upstairs. Among the great unthinkable things of this world, one of those near the head of the list would be to hurry a presumable Old Who's Who (Eton). As a result, our friends got into the house two days before Christmas.

Then the lady we are writing about sat down and had a quiet cry, because their Christmas-tree lights didn't have the right sort of plug and anyway she didn't know about power points. (You know what a "power point" is? A power point is an electrical outlet where, if you plug in your electric razor thinking it's an *ordinary* electrical outlet they come around next day and take you away in a box. You know what a "heated towel rail" is? That's a thing which, if you back into it after the bath, and the central heating is actually working, you get a nasty surprise, not to mention a painful welt.)

Finally, the man we are writing about said, "Now we're in, you might say we're flush with success," and the lady said, "If you don't want to go around with a plumber's helper stuck to your head, you'll give that up." Which he did.

Short, sad and very true (oh, how perishing true) verse

On nights damp and dreary
An open fire's cheery,
For looks there is little can beat it;
It chases out gloom
And does much for a room
—Except, of course, properly heat it.

It's a plane, it's a bird, it's . . . no, it's super-sun

A large bright object has been observed in the sky over London at frequent intervals lately, occasioning, in the beginning, no end of wonderment and awe. Turned out to be the sun.

All of a sudden it's spring.

There are yellow, almost orange crocuses out in the parks, and by every Tube station there's a flower-seller with his barrow draped in mats of artificial grass, selling daffodils and tulips, snowdrops from Cornwall, and anemones and violets.

Of course, the way the smog has been, all this may have been going on for weeks without anyone's having noticed.

The sun has been shining, it's warm and it's bright,
The trees are in bud in the square,
The winter miasma has gone overnight,
There's something quite fine in the air;
If that weren't enough to dispel any gloom,
The barrow boys' barrows have burst into bloom,
And these are the reasons you're hearing me sing,
All of a sudden, a sudden, a sudden,
All of a sudden it's spring.

All of a sudden, too, it turns out that much of a correspondent's research has to be done out of doors, just wandering around looking at things—such as researching the walk between the House of Commons and Bouverie Street, where his office is.

You come down the Embankment, keeping a sharp eye on the movement of oil barges on the Thames and the way the seagulls wheel about making a-a-a-king sounds, and catching up on such things as the inscription at the foot of Cleopatra's Needle telling how they got it there. (Very interesting story that; must look into it more one day.)

Beside the Embankment as you go on, there are a couple of slices of park where hundreds of office workers take their lunches in the shadow of such worthies as William Tyndale, b. (for born) 1484, first translator of the *New Testament* into English from Greek, and Sir Arthur Sullivan with a disconsolate Muse clutching at his knees.

> Platoons of stenographers, squadrons of clerks
> In hundreds at noontime deploy
> With paper-wrapped lunches to benches in parks
> (There's one just behind the Savoy);
> And on the Embankment the parapet's lined
> With people just sunning, rejoicing to find
> Here it's just March and, oh, wonderful thing,
> All of a sudden, a sudden, a sudden,
> All of a sudden it's spring.

Under Charing Cross Bridge, which is not the most felicitous location, there are several small restaurants. One of them has a sign making this reasonable declaration of policy: "People bringing their own food cannot be accommodated here."

A couple of doors down there is a shop where anyone could put together a five-foot shelf of decidedly strange reading: *History of Torture Through the Ages. Under the Lash. Selected Writings of De Sade. History of Corporal Punishment.*

Everyone to his own taste.

You cut back to the Embankment through another slice of park, and the parapet and the rail of Waterloo Bridge are lined with people intently studying such novel sights as Scott's ship, the *Discovery,* which has been where it is for only a few decades; the ship of the Honourable Company of Master Mariners; the *Chrysanthemum,* which is a Merchant Navy training centre; and HMS *President,* an aged vessel with a pile of miscellaneous gear on the jetty beside it,

92

including some radar and an electric fan. There's nothing like spring to cause people to stand like that and watch the water and the old ships that they have seen a hundred times before.

> A pigeon sits sunning on Nelson's cockade,
> The jets chalk white marks in the sky,
> While there in Hyde Park the big prams are arrayed
> With nannies in grey standing by;
> And down in the Strand, the crowds back from lunch
> Are wooed with "Anemones, sixpence a bunch."
> There's an air of a festival, blowout, or fling;
> All of a sudden, a sudden, a sudden,
> All of a sudden it's spring.

So that's the way you get back to the office from the House of Commons. And by the time you do, you're so full of zest at the idea of the smog's having gone and of spring's having arrived, that for fully five minutes you can't shut an eye.

Hey, take a look at us all of a sudden we're historical

The Ministry of Housing and Local Government has been casting an eye around the country, looking for buildings which, because of some special merit, ought not to be carelessly demolished or drastically altered.

Recently it did the City of Westminster where the Queen, the Prime Minister, and various others of us live—it's a big place—and the other morning's mail brought a letter saying, "Important. This communication affects your property."

Thrilled? It's hard to put into words. There you are, one day complaining about the open pipe that cascades the next higher tenant's overflow bathwater down your back window, and the next you find yourself living in a place listed as having special architectural or historical interest. It takes some getting used to.

Suddenly, we are squarely in a class with Cleopatra's Needle, St. James's Palace, Westminster Hall, the house that Disraeli lived in, the Royal Albert Hall, a decorative lamp-post, and the monument to Jan

Christian Smuts in Parliament Square. All of these made it onto the list with us, as did Buckingham Palace.

All anyone can hope is that the street out front will not become clogged with staring tourists.

The oldest of the buildings and monuments appearing in the Westminster list is Cleopatra's Needle, which the British liberated from Egypt in 1877. It was built, or assembled, or whatever is done with obelisks, about 1,500 years ago, and stood in front of the Great Temple of Heliopolis. (This interesting fact happens to be at fingertip because the finger the tip belongs to is stuck in an encyclopedia.)

The newest building or monument is the Smuts statue which dates from 1956. In between come Westminster Hall, which was built in 1097 by William Rufus and re-roofed by Richard II (there'd been a fire); the fourteenth century Jewel House of the Palace of Westminster which has a moat around it with trout in it; the remains of the monastic buildings around the Abbey; No. 10 Downing Street; and St. James's Palace.

And, of course, us and the lamp-post.

For rich, satisfying protests it's Aldermaston every time

What passes for a protest march in Canada is fifty people slouching uncertainly and self-consciously outside the doors of the Parliament buildings with placards on sticks.

The art of protest marching is not much more highly developed in the United States, although the great Civil Rights march in Washington in August, 1963, was a classic example of what a march ought to be.

France, or at least Paris, does it rather better. An item which any connoisseur of the march as a political art form might regret having missed was the 1958 march of the Left along the Boulevard Voltaire from the Place de la Nation to the Place de la République. That march was a veritable river of people, bright with flags and clamorous with songs and slogans.

The thing against which the marchers marched was the imminent coming to power of General Charles de Gaulle. While aesthetically satisfying, the march could hardly be called a conspicuous political success, the General being where he is these days.

But for sheer meaty goodness, for a nourishing protest march like mother (a suffragette) used to make, it would be hard to beat the annual Easter weekend London-Aldermaston march. The Aldermaston march has been held for seven years now and if it hasn't succeeded in ridding the world, or Britain, of nuclear weapons, neither has anyone or anything, including snow, hail, or the dark of night, succeeded in discouraging the marchers from their self-appointed round.

One day the Aldermaston march will come to be called the *traditional* Aldermaston march, whereupon it will be enshrined in the national folkways and guaranteed continuance long after everyone has forgotten what it was about. Like Maypole dancing. This is the way it goes:

Propped against the hindquarters of one of the lions on the pedestal of Nelson's column, the man with the red armband marked Chief Marshal was briefing his subordinate marshals, in laborious detail, on their duties.

While still in the square—Trafalgar Square, the time 10:30 a.m.—they would endeavour to get the marchers in order by saying, "Get in threes, please get in threes." The marshal obviously had never been a corporal, otherwise the instruction would have been, "Arright now, get fell in."

They would also see to the proper stationing of the people who would carry the banners.

How, asked a marshal, would one contact the chief marshal while on the march? The chief marshal gave a sound indicating he had almost forgotten an important matter.

"I will be in a car," he said. "Usually when I have any instructions to give I will write them out on a page from this pad" (he held the pad aloft so that there could be no mistake about it) "and I will give messages in writing so as to insure against misinterpretation."

The march to Aldermaston, fifty miles away in Berkshire, was due to move off at 11:30.

On the other side of the monument from where the chief marshal was briefing his generals, a fierce-eyed woman was lecturing a group around her, mostly, it appeared, on the evils of United States foreign policy.

95

"This is the Communist Party," cried a second woman from the fringe of the group, and all eyes swivelled around. "I thought you would be here. Remember Hungary?"

"What about Suez," said the first, cutting her off.

The challenger came back in full stride with a remark about a "lot of soft heads." Then she said, "Let the Russians march; let them march in Russia about the bomb."

The other, meanwhile, had turned away. "I may be vulgar," she was saying (apropos of what it would be difficult to guess), "but I am honest. What about the coloured people in South Africa? What about that, eh? Damned cheek it is."

A U.S. broadcaster with a tape-recorder was having a thin time of it.

An unshaven, bleary-eyed little fellow who looked as if he had slept the night under a table said vaguely, "If you'll just give us back Piccadilly Circus we'll be happy."

A Scot said, "The Americans are going to give the Nazis atom bombs, hydrogen bombs."

Another man volunteered the startling information that the Girl Scouts in Americker were collecting money to help set up soup kitchens.

By the time the speeches started at 11:00, the crowd had become thick—two or three thousand. Most of the marchers were young, in their teens and early twenties, the males running heavily to tentative beards.

A group of teen-age girls in beanies, jeans, windbreakers and loafers posed for a cameraman, their wavering banners declaring: "Youth Says: We Want Peace." There were banners by the dozen, crudely handmade and bearing such inscriptions as: "Shall Our Children Die?" "Would You Drop an H-Bomb?" "Let Britain Give a Lead," and "From Fear to Sanity."

A hawk-faced, middle-aged woman elbowed her way to the front of the crowd, her eyes on the cameras. "This will go all over the world, dear," she was telling her friend. "They won't keep this in a corner of the *Evening News*."

The chief marshal made an announcement that all marshals were to return to the west side of the plinth. "The west side of the plinth is this side; I am pointing there now."

The hawk-faced woman passed approval on Bertrand Russell, one of the patrons of the march. "Oh, Bertrand Russell's the man,"

96

she told her friend. "They have him in *The Sunday Times* and *The Observer* and everywhere. Oh, he's a good man."

Canon L. J. Collins of St. Paul's, another of the patrons, told the crowd that one of the first things that had to be done after the march was to impress upon the Government that the marchers represented the views of the majority of the people of Britain. The march was a beginning, not an end.

Michael Foot, a radical editor and parliamentarian, roused the crowd and sent the pigeons fluttering with a roaring speech, the theme of which was that the rulers must be made to listen.

The speeches over, a young man in the crowd was making a defensive argument to some people around him. "I think Britain ought to give it up," he was saying, "but not the United States. The Russians have it."

"Tripe," said a woman loudly.

"Shut up," said her husband.

The march began.

A young girl in high heels, black stockings and tight skirt; a young couple with a baby in a pram; men in hiking clothes with knapsacks; a party of Scottish dancers, the men in velvet jackets and carrying swords; sincere pacifists; thoughtful men; frightened men; Communist party men playing a party game; teenagers on a weekend's fun; nuts; publicity-seekers; and people who simply wanted company—perhaps a thousand of them marching through the Good Friday streets.

Natty gents' furnishings
for all formal occasions

One day, the editor of *Tailor and Cutter,* who keeps a sharp, even censorious eye on the clothes that men wear, grieved in public about the way men dress for weddings, including, principally, their own.

The bride, he said, insisted upon a proper wedding gown, but the groom unfortunately, in very many cases, let the side down. The result was this:

"We see too often leering at us from the local photographer's show windows, the doleful solecism of the bride in white and the gauche young groom in a gent's natty summer suit (with silver papered carnation pinned to his lapel, ye gods)."

It was with the same thought of serving the common good that another of the great authorities on Clothes and the Man caused a despatch to be sent off post-haste, on learning that the bowler was making some modest inroads in Canada. Not that that upset him, but there was a suggestion that some men had been seen in brown, and even green (ye gods) bowlers. Choking back his nausea, he wrote:

It is to be hoped that the following general information on the wearing of hats will be received in the right spirit, as coming from someone who is not only located in the men's style centre of the world, but who himself enjoys some small reputation as the glass of fashion, and a pioneer—a pioneer whose introduction of the tweed cap with dinner jacket was received with widespread revulsion in Ottawa some years ago.

[A narrow lot, those Ottawa people, and set in their ways. . . . But we digress; the subject was bowlers, advice on the wearing of.]

As demonstrated by the Englishmen who wear them (which means every Englishman who suffers a twinge of guilt whenever he find himself turning to the *Daily Mirror* ahead of *The Times*), there are two places where the bowler may be worn, only one of which is on the head.

A systematic survey undoubtedly would show that 67 per cent of the Englishmen who wear bowlers do so on their right hand. These hats, one suspects, are bought by glove sizes. Come rain or shine, the bowler remains in the hand, in the ready position for meeting a lady or soliciting alms. (Very few bowler-wearers actually do solicit alms. A beggar in a bowler would be looked upon as putting on airs and getting above his station, and this would not be well regarded. There are traditions in these things.)

Assuming that the bowler is going to be worn on the head, it must be said at once that it is not put there haphazardly. It is not clapped down on the back of the head in the Front Page manner, nor is it worn tilted over one ear. The people who wear their bowlers at an angle not infrequently carry small black doctors' bags and are members of the Bookmakers' Protective Association.

The bowler is worn square and rather far forward on the brow. In fact, the brim may be allowed to rest on the bridge of the nose where it permits the wearer to see nothing above the level of his vest. This style is particularly favoured by Guards officers, whose off-duty uniform begins with the bowler. Guards officers *on* duty wear bearskin hats which come down to their noses, and it is believed that they develop a form of radar which leads them unseeingly, but unerringly, in their off-duty hours, to debutantes, champagne, and the other essentials of the young Guards officer's life.

There is a place and time to wear the bowler and a place and time not to; it is not worn indiscriminately. A gentleman coming up to the City five days of the week in a bowler would never think of doing so if he were to come up on the Saturday or Sunday. If he dropped into the office on Saturday morning to open his mail he would wear—if he had an ounce of sporting blood in him—something with a little dash to it, perhaps with the brim rolled sharply up at the sides, Robin Hoodish, "wiv a bit uv a fevver in the band," as one of the lower orders might say.

For walking the dog, a tweed or felt cap is called for; for shooting, a tweed hat or a deerstalker such as Sherlock Holmes wore, but preferably much, much hairier. An afternoon at the races demands a grey topper, and evening wear, of course, a black one. A beret is the thing for being devilish on the Continent.

But a green bowler, ye gods.

Y*ou always know it's summer by the blue-mould on your shoes*

It was, as the English say, unusual weather for June. Before that it had been unusual weather for January, February, March, April and May. It is one of the great truths that the weather here usually is unusual, but in June it was more unusual than usual.

Down at Kew, where the weatherman apparently keeps his measuring basins, they recorded 4.2 inches of rain during June. Except for 1903, which must have been the rainiest June since Noah was in the boatbuilding business, there hadn't been a rainier June since man emerged from the ooze.

> There's a dismal damping downpour down at Kew,
> There's a doleful dripping drizzle down at Kew,
> In the month of sun and flowers
> They'd a record lot of hours
> When they suffered summer showers down at Kew.

Rain? The BBC began its nightly weather summary one night with the solemn announcement: "There was only a little rain today." That, the way things were, was News.

> There's a soaking summer shower down at Kew,
> There's a silly soggy sprinkle down at Kew,
> And the everlasting cinch is
> That each Londoner just flinches
> As he thinks of June in inches down at Kew.

Ascot got rained on. Garden parties got rained on. The Queen got rained on at the Trooping of the Colour. At Wimbledon, the latter-day practitioners of Sphairistike kept landing on their backs on the sacred but soggy and slippery turf of the Centre Court.

> There's a chilly clammy cloudburst down at Kew,
> There's a constant cursed cascade down at Kew,
> But our hopes accept no fetter
> Maybe now we'll get it better,
> For it couldn't be much wetter, down at Kew.

Finally, a London newspaper published a cartoon which depicted a farmer sitting on a horse, belly deep in a pond, shouting to a holiday family in a rowboat: "If you lot don't mind, this happens to be a field of wheat!"

Speak up, Thomas Edison, they haven't heard you yet

Sometimes, sitting here with my thumb in my mouth, I wonder about things.

I wonder, for instance, about the distrust of the natives—an essentially simple and childlike people—toward the box that speaks like a man, otherwise known as the telephone.

Alexander Graham Bell, or Don Ameche for that matter, would have wept.

Telephones are all right for calling people to ask about their health, and to exchange pleasantries, but telephones are *not* all right for doing business by, except perhaps for fly-by-nights and other insubstantial elements of the community.

Business is done by letter, as for instance:

Once upon a time, a Canadian, at whose identity I can only hint by a modest fluttering of the eyelids, received a letter from the Conservative Central Office asking him to say how many press tickets he wished for a Conservative women's conference.

Among his fervent desires, then or ever, the desire to sit and listen to a gaggle of Tory women in full cry would come rather far down the list—but duty, duty.

He telephoned Abbey 9000, Conservative headquarters, asked for the press office, gave his name, and said he would have one (1). All of this was duly digested at the other end—in any event there was a seemingly attentive silence—and then:

"Would you mind letting us have a letter on that?"

"Why?"

"It would really be most helpful if you would."

"Why?"

"We really should have a letter."

So much for the Conservative women (may their flowered hats wither).

Then there was the case of a man who called his lawyer to ask how matters were progressing on a property transaction which had been going on since shortly after the departure of the Romans.

"I shall be writing you today about that," said the lawyer.

And he did.

He wrote to say that the situation was unchanged from the last time he wrote.

I wonder about a lot of other things, too. But after wondering about Englishmen and the telephone for a while, I find that I have to go away and lie down.

How clouded was my crystal ball
(it didn't count on Charles de Gaulle)

There'll be coq-au-vin in tea-shops,
Fish and chips in Montparnasse,
There'll be bratwurst sold in Oireland,
And Italians drinking Bass.

There'll be sucking up of pastas,
In the Northern fjord ports,
And in bosky Holland polders,
They'll eat rich Vienna tortes.

There'll be crofters in the Highlands,
Downing fat Burgundian snails,
There'll be miners eating paté,
Down in Tonnypandy, Wales.

There'll be ivory-skinned Marquesas
Spooning cups of jellied eels,
And Greeks consuming Guinness,
With their frozen TV meals.

There'll be no more national cuisine,
But an international stew,
As they all grow rich and blasé
When the Common Market's through.

Common Market Revisited

When Britain tried to join the Six,
The five said, yes, the one said, nix,
"You don't belong with us at all,
Or so say I," said Charles de Gaulle.

P*in a rose on my middy, mother,*
for I am a girl of the realm

It was the pure mischance of discovering the existence of a league
of non-smokers dedicated to reducing the number of public places
where non-smokers are likely to be smoked at, that opened up the
whole numbing subject of the group-forming proclivities of the
natives of these islands.

The proclivities are considerable. It may be true, as it is alleged,
that two English castaways could live side by side for years without
exchanging a word, simply because they had not been introduced. If
it is so, it is a safe bet that if someone performed that simple office
the pair would form a League for the Preservation and Rehabilita-
tion of Distressed Mariners.

The London telephone directory lists eighty-one societies, including the Society for Distributing the Holy Scriptures to the Jews,
the Society for Friendship with Bulgaria, the Society for the Protection of Animals in North Africa, and the Society of Friends of Foreigners in Distress.

There is also a handful of leagues, including the League of
French Animal Welfare, which turns out to be a close neighbour of
the Society for Protection of Animals in North Africa. Undoubtedly,
at one time, these two were prone to jurisdictional disputes (to which
society would a maltreated Foreign Legion horse have appealed, for
example?) but events would now seem to have taken care of that.

But it is *Whitaker's Almanack,* that treasury of miscellaneous
facts, which reveals in their wondrous variety the causes to which the
natives of these islands can be persuaded to rally.

It seems that there are some fifteen hundred societies and institutions in England, so there is a cause for just about every taste, from
that of the person who worries about the welfare of pit ponies (Pit
Ponies Protection Society, 1927) to the advocate of a proportional
representation system of voting (Proportional Representation Society,
1844). There is an Anti-Slavery League, a British Goat Society, a
British Vigilance Association (which sounds terribly stern), and an
International Bureau for the Suppression of Traffic in Persons (which
sounds terribly worthy). There is also a Cave Research Group
of Great Britain, a Cereals and Baltic Friendly Society (an odd mix-

103

ture; a sort of buy-a-cream-of-wheat-breakfast-for-an-Estonian sort of society), an Egypt Exploration Society, a Society for the Assistance of Ladies in Reduced Circumstances (a lovely name, redolent of lavender, lace and bank overdrafts), and a Monumental Brass Society, which presumably is interested in large brass objects, and not in people with unpleasantly aggressive personalities.

What do they all do? Well, the British Vigilance Association, which might be a sort of counterpart to the Birch Society but isn't, engages in the gentle work of meeting young girls arriving in London from other countries and sheltering them. The aim of the League of Welldoers, as enunciated by the founder who went by the delightful name of H. Lee J. Jones, is "to feed, clothe, shelter and cheer those in need, irrespective of creed." Not an unworthy objective, at that. The Girls of the Realm Guild has two branches, the senior of which is dedicated to providing professional training for daughters of gentlefolk who are in need. The junior branch (which, bless us, is known as the Fairy Ring) assists, with school fees and incidental expenses, young daughters of gentlefolk who need help. (The process by which *gentlefolk* are identified from what presumably are known as *ungentlefolk* is not stated.)

There used to be a Society for Improving the Condition of the Labouring Classes, but it changed its name to the 1830 Housing Society. The date referred to was the date on which a still earlier predecessor, the Labourer's Friend Society, was founded. (That other friend of the labourer, the Labour Party, has also had to make adjustments. The improvement in the condition of the Labouring Classes has been such that an undue number of the said classes—at least from the Labour point of view—have come to suffer the illusion that they are Tories.)

The China Association exists to promote trade with China (and bad cess to the State Department in Washington) and also to keep old China hands in touch with affairs and with one another. The Anti-Slavery Society chips away at the remaining enclaves of slavery in the world.

For the joiner who may not qualify for the Fairy Ring, or feels that meeting foreign girls at railway stations is hardly his thing, or lacks a connection with China, or finds himself disinterested in stamping out the slave traffic—in other words, for reformers of a thoroughly selfish bent—there's always the Society of Friends of Wine. It's to be found in Vintner's Place.

104

M_y *pen is like a lissom leg and my seat is kumfydry*

Anthropologically, there are two basic types of Englishmen.

The first is the Farmer Type: square, apple-cheeked, stout, stolid, epitomized in the figure of John Bull. In the pure form, this type is to be found in corduroys, sloshing about with rubber boots on his feet, a pipe in his mouth and a pig under each arm. Over the centuries the Farmer Type, in all ranks, has been very good at fighting wars and going out to populate the colonies, two occupations for which there have been frequent calls on his services largely due to the machinations of Type Two.

This is what may be called the Foreign Office Type. The true specimen of this type will be found to be tall, concave, the least bit languid, and to preface most of his utterances with, "I mean to say . . . ." He is a worshipper of the intellect, which he knows flourishes in his homeland as nowhere else on earth. In fact, if caught off guard after midnight and after the eighth glass, he may admit to some doubt that it flourishes anywhere else at all, least of all in Americker. He places no great store by material things, and is faintly contemptuous of Americans, all of whom do. When he thinks of rewards at all, he thinks in terms of a title which may be translated into directorships, a Rolls-Royce, a good address, and similar intellectual stimulae.

Needless to say, there are Farmer types in bowler hats going off to the City every day with pigskin briefcases where the pigs were originally intended to be, and there are Foreign Office types pitching manure—some of them not even in the Foreign Office. But regardless of occupation or deviation from true outward form, the basic characteristics of the two types remain.

This established, what I want to know is where, in a population made up of stolid, let's-have-no-frippery farmers, and others to whom the frivolous is an intellectual affront, do the sprites come from who perform the fairywork that is to be found in British commerce?

For sheer makes-you-want-to-gag cuteness, commercial nomenclature in this country takes a lot of beating. One day, in the Lyons Corner House at Charing Cross, where I was engaged in a cheeseburger debauch, a young woman on the next stool ordered "a Wimpy,

105

a Yankee, and a Strawberry Whipsy." This produced, in addition to a sharp diminution in the appetite of her neighbour, a hamburger, a doughnut sort of confection, and a pink milk shake. Leaving the waitress nothing for a tipsy, except the hasty advice that she leave while her reason remained intact, reporter left, resolved to go back to eating in pubs. There, at least, a pint of wallop remains a pint of wallop and a sausage is only a banger.

The London Transport Commission for these many moons has been advertising a sort of day-long around-London bus excursion which it is pleased to call a Red Rover. For all I know, the Red Rover trip may be fascinating, amusing, and educational, but it's difficult to think of anyone going to a wicket and asking for a Red Rover without also imagining the ticket-seller leaning out through the bars, playfully slapping the tripper's wrist, and saying: "Oooh, I just know you're going to have *such* fun."

A firm which makes a soft drink called Idris chooses to advertise its products with drawings of a small square holding a bottle and proclaiming that, for him, it's "Idris when I's dri." Arrgh. There's also a sort of iced confection on a stick that goes by the name of Iced Lolly.

But it was while sitting in the lobby of the Grand Hotel in Oran, Algeria, waiting for a taxi (of all unlikely places and occupations), that the horrible truth dawned. This tendency to archness isn't confined to consumer advertising, where a degree of preciosity is perhaps to be expected, but also extends to the sales messages of hard-headed Midlands manufacturers to hard-headed merchants. The sole item of reading material in the lobby turned out, for some unfathomable reason, to be a February issue of the *Mercantile Guardian,* a fat magazine catering to sellers and buyers of British goods.

The ads of this solid, no-nonsense publication brought to light the fact that George MacLellan & Co., of Maryhill, Glasgow, offers in the markets of the world the Kumfydry reversible bicycle seat cover. No more wet bottom with the good old Kumfydry reversible bicycle seat cover; just turn it over and there you are . . . Kumfydry.

Dr. Sebel & Co. Ltd., West St., Erith, Kent, markets what it calls "the Fold-a-Bye Writing Desk and Chair," and New Hygiene Ltd., London, has Wham "the pleasant insecticide." In case the insecticide proves to be innocuous as well as pleasant, flies can be made to drop at the wave of the slogan, which is, "Wham it, dammit!"

Cotswold Plastics Ltd., offers what undoubtedly is a very big item in Port Said and similar cultural retreats, "Temptation . . . this brilliant ballpoint pen shaped enticingly like a lovely lissom leg."

106

Dirty British coaster with a salt-caked smoke stack,
Butting through the Channel in the mad March days,
With a cargo of Kumfydrys,
Fold-a-Byes, leg pens,
Wham cans, Idris, and cheap tin tways.

It's every man for himself, Masefield; the leprechauns have taken over and not an Englishman remains alive. Not in advertising, anyway.

Of leather breeches, benches, and soggy, soggy landlords

In late June, London elects its own sheriffs and a number of other officials, including four ale conners who are paid £10 a year for testing beer, but don't—except perhaps privately. So far as is known, they don't even have the leather pants which, as everyone knows, are indispensable to proper beer testing.

In the days when there were some 750 inns, taverns and ale-houses in the City—that's the business section, not all of London— twenty-six conners used to go around, pouring beer on benches, sitting in it with their leather breeches, and seeing if they stuck.

If they stuck, the beer was strong enough. If they didn't, the landlord was forced to drink as much of his brew as he could hold and the rest was then poured over him.

It's just as well the practice was discontinued or nowdays there would be a lot of wet landlords.

Rain, rain, beautiful rain everyone's sloshingly happy again

Just at the moment when the country appeared ready to crack under the strain of a long succession of sunny, dry days, the weather has turned a little miserable. There has been fog in the mornings and rain several times during the day, and once more the natives can hold their heads up and smile.

There was one traffic jam in England over last weekend. It was outside Sheffield and was caused by joyous people flocking out to see how the rains were filling up the municipal reservoir. Everywhere else, people deprived of any such glorious excuse to get out into the rain huddled happily by their fires, practising for the winter which, with any luck, will be absolutely filthy.

If it's not, there won't be enough ships to hold the emigrants.

This past summer, which was the best in two hundred years, caused a lot of discontented muttering before it was over, and if people have to endure a comfortable winter on top of it, a lot of them are going to start saying they'd be as well off in Canader or Austrailier or one of those places. At least, they'll say to one another, "If you can't be cold and damp, you might as well go out to Canader where at least it gets *proper* cold." And if they go, and their first winter turns out to be mild, they'll feel cheated and the *People* will carry stories on how the Canadian Meteorological Service hornswoggled a family from Tooting into believing that in Canada they could find a decent standard of climatological discomfort.

When the best summer in two hundred years began, people faced up to it by assuring themselves and others that "This won't last; you'll see." But it did, and by August when holiday time came around, tempers were wearing a little thin.

People taking holidays in Britain set off without their usual feeling of anticipation. Given a wet summer, like almost any summer you care to name, a man can set off brimful of confidence that the weather's bound to get better during his two weeks.

When it turns out not to do so . . . well, there's always a warm sweater and the pub, and, well, that's England, isn't it?

Back in town, glowing from exposure to the wet, within and without, he has something to look forward to.

"Not another holiday at home for me, old boy. No bloody fear. South of France for me next year, you wait and see."

This past summer the post-holiday conversations tended to be rather lugubrious:

"Good holiday, old boy?"

"Sunshine every day. Stifling hot."

"Strange summer, wasn't it?"

"We're going to pay for this, you mark my words."

108

If domestic holidayers were robbed of their sense of anticipation, those going to the Continent were robbed of the very reason for going. An Englishman goes to the Continent for "a bit of sun." Certainly he doesn't go there to eat a lot of strange food, sleep in strange beds, suffer ghastly experiences with strange plumbing (it is a popular delusion that British plumbing works and other plumbing doesn't; actually the travelling Englishman simply misses the exercise of chinning himself on a chain), and most particularly he doesn't go to the Continent to be messed about by a lot of foreigners who don't even speak English. When the English summer is being so exceptional, what reason has he for going at all when he can get a bit of sun at home? None. But his bookings were made in February, and, upper lip stiff, he presses on with the indomitable spirit that built an Empire.

But now, all's well again; it's raining. The other morning, one of the popular papers which recognizes a heart-warming story when it sees it, headed a piece on Page One: "In Comes the Skid Season." Slippery roads had caused hundreds of accidents over the weekend, it reported, rubbing its editorial hands with the satisfaction of knowing that things were back to normal.

A woman columnist in another paper rejoiced that now the hot weather was gone one could again take a drink for the sake of a drink—not just to slake thirst, but "for that warm feeling in the pit of one's tum" (her words, be assured, not mine).

One of these nights, a fog the colour and consistency of chicken gravy will settle down just at the time of the homeward rush. Lines of cars ten miles long will be stalled, suburban trains will run late, and the newspapers will report with immense satisfaction to their satisfied readers that tomorrow promises to be infinitely worse.

As for me, I'm busy spinning a cocoon.

The good little fairy birds are strictly for the birds

Here in England, Christmas is the time of the pantomimes and they are ever such jolly fun. One day I was sitting in the circle at the Coliseum, exposing myself to the wondrous enchantment of "Aladdin," when some little perisher in a box above dropped, or threw, the major portion of his Eskimo pie. Oh, they are jolly.

When the pantomimes are on, every father with a drop of honest red blood in his veins faces up to the fact that life is not just one mad round of pleasure and, oozing bogus bonhomie, takes whatever offspring may be about the place down to the West End.

Me, I've got two drops. The time I speak of, I had been twice, in three days—there's raw courage for you—as the custodian of the resident pantomime addict, Christopher.

In addition to the wondrous enchantment of "Aladdin" at the Coliseum we went to the Players' Theatre, under the tracks at Charing Cross, where the offering for the happy, happy holiday season was "Babes in the Woods and the Good Little Fairy Birds."

That was all one bill; "Babes in the Woods and the Good Little Fairy Birds." Even now, merely to write the words is to bring once more the bile—pardon, smile—to my lips.

Cor blimey, that was a double bill for you. Triple bill, in fact, for there was a harlequinade following, with Harlequin, and Columbine, and Pantaloon with gouty foot, and Smeraldina, who was, and perhaps still is, a poodle, and God knows who else. (Smeraldina was played by Miss Sheila Bernette, who, only a few moments before, was the fairy bird cuckoo, and it all became a trifle confusing, particularly if one was fortunate enough to be able to drop off now and again.)

The resident pantomime addict found "Babes in the Woods" woefully deficient in wickedness and the "Good Little Fairy Birds" for the birds.

"Whaddaya mean, there weren't enough wicked people in it?" said his jovial old Pa as they left. "What about the uncle who hired the two men to take the children into the woods and kill them?"

"I mean really wicked people," said the pantomime addict. "Witches and things."

It's television wot's done it, that's wot. When I was that age, one prolonged exposure to a stage uncle wicked enough to hire a pair of thugs to do in his innocent nephew and niece would have been good for a week's run of technicolour nightmares.

For the sake of those who have led sheltered lives and have never been exposed to the intricacies of a pantomime plot (a hideously inadequate word in the circumstances, "plot") we shall now briefly sketch the plot of "Babes in the Woods and the Good Little Fairy Birds."

110

First of all, there's Sir Rowland Macassar, the uncle in question, and his wife who is, of course, Aunty Macassar. (By George, they don't make witty ones like that any more. It's a play on words, like.) Uncle and Aunty Macassar are short at the bank and the only way they can see out of their difficulties is to despatch the two moppets, who are heirs to the considerable fortune of their presumed-to-be-late Papa, who is thought to have perished in a wreck at sea.

To make a long story short—an act of Christian mercy which nobody performed for me—they hire two thugs to knock the kids off; one of the thugs, in the very nick, admits to being their lost parent; the remaining thug is done in; Uncle Macassar is forgiven his lapse; Papa marries the kids' schoolteacher; and everyone, including the good little fairy birds (who follow), lives happily ever after.

Yucht.

And so to "Aladdin." Now "Aladdin" is, and always was, more the classical pantomime, in a big theatre, with lavish sets, costumes in all the primary colours, and several acres of jewels.

Every adult, of course, knows the story of Aladdin, but once that handicap has been overcome there is no real difficulty in following the entirely unrelated tale that unfolds on the stage. You see, there's the Wicked Magician from Morocco who goes to Peking seeking Aladdin, who is a poor but honest street peddler who falls in love with the Princess . . . but then, let's not spoil it.

Naturally, being a pantomime, a male comedian plays a dame part, in this case a red-headed old dame, the Widow Twankee, Aladdin's mother. Also, being a pantomime, there were numbers of young dames who were all dame, to keep the daddies from drifting off to Slumberland. There was, for instance, a scene in the Princess's baths, which attracted whistles from some of the more mature boys in the galleries. "Look," said Christopher, "ladies." Look? So who's not looking?

Of course, being a pantomime, the villain got hissed and booed. At one point there was the wicked villain Abanazar ("a wicked magician from Morocco") ranting at Aladdin while hissing filled the theatre like the sound of leaking radiators.

"I'll get revenge," said the wicked villain, in his most wickedly villainous tones.

And a piping voice from high up in the gods came back, "Aww, knock it orf."

It was about that time that the kid in the box above dropped his Eskimo pie and the resident pantomime addict said for the twenty-

111

seventh time, "When are they going to get started on the real story?"

And his parent said: "I didn't know you knew Aladdin. Is it in one of your books?"

"No. I saw it on 'Popeye.' "

Aladdin? On "Popeye"?

Songs, dances and funny sayings, have shears: will travel

On King's Road in Chelsea, downstairs under a tobacco store, there's a small barbershop. The barber has just recently increased the price of kids' haircuts to three shillings and sixpence—about half-a-dollar—which is not a lot, but it's more than before.

He didn't say it was because the price of scissors had gone up, or because kids were growing tougher hair. He didn't say anything except that from now on kids' haircuts would cost three-and-six. It could be a case of a man trying deliberately to price himself out of the market.

That day, a client, recently turned seven, was in the chair. The barber listened patiently and said, "uh-huh, uh-huh," from time to time as the Young Client told him what he had got for Christmas, what he had got for the birthday that followed soon after, how he was doing at school, and various personal anecdotes calculated to stupefy on impact.

When the barber's eye had taken on the glazed look of a cold fried egg, the Young Client said, "Did you hear about the kidnapping in California?"

"No," said the barber, visibly regretful that it had happened so far from present surroundings. "What happened?"

"They woke him up," said the Y.C.

Snip, snip, snip.

"What was that you said?" said the barber, warily.

"I said did-you-hear-about-the-kidnapping-in-California-and-you-said-no-what-happened-and-I-said-they-woke-him-up," said the Y.C.

"Ha, ha," said the barber.

Snip, snip, snip.

112

"What time is it when the clock strikes fourteen times?" said the Y.C.

"I give up," said the barber. "What time is it?"

"Time to get it fixed."

"Ha, ha," said the barber.

"How much," said the Young Client, "are 5Q and 5Q?"

"5Q and 5Q?" said the barber. "Ten Q."

"You're welcome."

"Ha, ha," said the barber. "You sure have a lot of them, haven't you? Where did you get them; out of a book?"

"Yes, it was a book I got for Christmas called *Play-and-Draw* and it's got lots of . . . . Do you know that you can't hang a man with a beard?"

"No," said the barber. "Why can't you hang a man with a beard?"

"You've got to use a rope."

"Very funny," said the barber.

Shortly after that he put down his scissors, undid the cloth around the kid's neck, slid him down to the floor, and announced that kids' haircuts were now three-and-six.

On top of that, the kid got the lousiest haircut in London.

Yes, and what do I get for paying my union dues?

NEWS ITEM: Christine Keeler and Mandy Rice-Davies became literary lions in Britain with their collections of bedtime stories—or Tories, if you prefer.

Christine, I'm afraid, you get much better paid
(And I trust you won't take this as slighting)
Than most of us do, who are rather less new
At this business of earning by writing.

If this seems a gripe at a novice in type
I assure you it's far from my meaning,
For truly one sees that to sell expertise
For much less would be rather demeaning.

113

But still I'll admit that it pains me a bit
To reflect on the mountain of stories
For which in the year I'll get less than you, dear,
For telling a tale on some Tories.

What's more, I'll bet your hours were better, too.

A *word for nose-thumbers,*
may their ranks never dwindle

Some people collect coins, some collect stamps, some collect bottle-caps, matchbook covers, old railway time tables, cigarette cards with pictures of old automobiles, or the batting averages of right-handed, blue-eyed Caucasian hitters in the National League. I collect snippets from the bottoms of columns in the newspapers, particularly snippets about people in revolt.

No conscientious collector of such snippets could pass up the London press; there is no richer source of items about vigorous nose-thumbers.

Item: In Jersey, a man walked into the income tax office, plunked down a loaf of bread, put his coat over it, topped these with his income tax form, and stalked out after having declared, "There's the bread out of my mouth and the coat off my back; now you've got the lot."

Item: A correspondent of *The Guardian* reported finding among other graffiti on the wall of a Sheffield public lavatory this cheerfully thumb-to-nose greeting: "A Merry Christmas to all our readers."

Item: In Coventry, a woman, married to a sixty-six-year-old man who regularly dyed his hair to make the girls think he was younger, took to putting peroxide in her husband's hair oil.

Item: At Bolney, Sussex, a postman, plainly in revolt, arrived with the Christmas mail, drove his truck into the doors of a shed, fell out, staggered to the door to hand the housewife a bundle of letters (only two of which proved to be for her), then climbed into the truck on the passenger side where he sat asking, "Where's the wheel?"

Item: In London, a man had a simple answer when he was ques-

114

tioned about his failure to fill in unemployment insurance forms. "I don't need these cards," he said. "I get my living thieving."

Item: A Fleet Street bookseller, in an obvious gesture of rebellion against narrow convention, displayed among the volumes on cricket, sailing, fishing and wood-turning on his shelves marked "Sports and Hobbies," a volume by a Dr. Eustace Chasser entitled, *Women.*

Rather more difficult to classify, but certainly reflecting a certain tough-minded unwillingness to accept things as they are (or seem to be), was the item about a London woman who set out to prove that sound percussion could affect the growth of plants. She claimed to have excited potted marigolds into increased growth and earlier flowering by doing the Indian Bharata Natyam dance in front of them every morning.

Finally, as an example of revolt by the well-ordered mind against an increasingly disordered world, there was the story of the woman in Nottingham who was awakened by a crashing noise downstairs at 5:00 a.m., and discovering a circus elephant in the doorway, left her husband to fend it off with the vacuum cleaner while she rushed to the police station where she announced: "We've an elephant in."

And the policeman said calmly: "Are you sure?"

OUTDOORS

The memoirs of a sport

The race is to the swift
which means the other one

It was Derby Day and of course one went. It is one of the things one does.

The Derby has been run now for more than 180 years and simply reeks of history, not to mention jellied eels, beer and moth balls. (Those grey toppers and clawhammer coats don't get aired every day of the week, you know.)

Derby Day dawned a typical English summer's day—threatening rain. Any more rain and it would have been the first running of the Derby with the horses on pontoons.

Not one to be put off by a touch of the damp, the eager correspondent, a long-standing student of the turf (Dufferin '48, with honours), sprang from his couch at the crack of 10:00 a.m. and was off.

Following is his chart:

11:00 Broke fast from front door and breezed six furlongs to Victoria Station, establishing new track record. Bought second-class return ticket—five-and-tuppence—and boarded 11:08 for Epsom Downs.

11:55 Epsom Downs Station. Plodded across Down, following cluster of people with picnic baskets. Race-goers? Sunday School picnic?

12:05 p.m. Arrived back of grandstand. Parking lot filled with Rolls-Royces and Bentleys and nobs in fancy suits. How many owned, how many hired from Moss Bros?

Passed up grandstand (£3), Barnard's stand (37s, 6d) made for infield (free). Infield filled with people, beer tents, ferris wheels, buses, cars, more people.

Listened to tout in sharp black suit, big red carnation in buttonhole, "I'm going to make a statement, and here's £100. The biggest mug in the world can bet them odds-on. What you got to know, my

119

father—and he was one of the biggest professional betters in the country—he always said, 'Never bet odds-on.' "

Wandered off thinking that if father could be found, might get the distilled essence of his wisdom. Instead encountered seedier-looking tout crying: "Don't all rush at once! I'm the Shilling-Shocker. I was up here at ha' past five this morning watching them gallop. If you don't know 'em, I can help you. I'm the Shilling-Shocker."

Looked the part.

12:50 Farther into infield, past ferris wheels, coconut shies, Sheena Queen of the Rats, and The Lovely Slave Girl Entombed with Living Death. Show labelled Strip Tease Girls, with the 's' on girls added in pencil; cast apparently recently enlarged. Sign says "Adults Only." Judging by the prospective clientele, an adult is anyone tall enough to reach up to the ticket window.

1:10 Lunch. Passed up Zwanenberg's Frankfurters, the Speedie Feedie Hastie Tastiest, and the jellied eels. A sunbathed washtubful of jellied eels looked most unappetizing—so much so almost gave up idea of lunch. For moment thought might give up breakfast, retroactively. So . . . cheese sandwich (two slices of cardboard enclosing piece cut from an inner tube).

1:15 Scanned bookies. Billy Cunningham, Prompt Payment, Civility; Percy (Always Pays) Jones; Alf Thomas, Civility and Security. Liked sound of that Security; can always make do without Civility.

Ten shillings on Belle Combattante, a hunch, having just returned from France.

1:45 Sighted first horse; biggish jockey in dark blue, gold braid on cap. Policeman. Made note to get seat in stands next time, or field glasses.

2:00 They're off.

Belle Combattante ran well. All other horses but one ran better.

Studied merry-go-round for form—Pettigrove's Twentieth Century Grand Gold Galloping Horses, the Ride to Suit All Ages, a Thrill of a Lifetime, the Pride of the South.

2:20 Bet five shillings on horse named Rosalea; nice name.

2:30 Rosalea turned out to have been named Rosalba, and not very fast runner. Fourth of five.

Listened to tout: "Some of the race-tracks I go to, I go by air. Some of them I go to, I go by car, my own car . . . . Up to four and five in the morning, drinking and smoking cigars." (Complaining or

120

boasting?) "No man in England knows more about it than I do. Two bob and I only hope you make as much money on the Derby as I have."

3:15 Place bet (£1; a fig for expense) on Alberta Blue in Derby. One of ours.

Looked on with a hundred thousand-odd others as the Queen in orange (apricot?) coat walks from paddock to stand with Queen Mother and Princess Margaret. Not a step more than a mile-and-a-half away.

3:20 Horses paraded. No can find Alberta Blue.

Horses at starting post, out of sight behind ferris wheels, girlie shows, mass of humanity in infield. Off! Sound of great excitement as horses make way around track. Presume that's what's going on.

Around Tattenham Corner. Alberta Blue, where are yo-o-o-u? Down the stretch it's Hard Ridden, Paddy's Point, Gamami. Finish in that order. Never once laid eyes on Alberta Blue from beginning to end.

Train to Victoria, sharing compartment with young American who said he'd had jellied eels and ice-cream for lunch; and a bottle of beer. Also said he was not feeling well.

Turned out not on train to Victoria. Dumped out at London Bridge to fight way home in rush-hour traffic. Wonder if can put pound on Alberta Blue, five shillings on Rosalba and ten shillings on Belle Combattante on expense account as research?

The Cadillac's only a symbol
but a Rolls is the thing for a gent

The first fact that must be put down in any comparative study of the place of the automobile in the society of Great Britain and North America is that in Britain there is a different attitude toward the car.

The car in North America is a success symbol. The successful executive's car is a great long thing, with flamboyant fins and square yards of chrome, the whole designed to proclaim to the world (and whisper assurance to the occupant) that he is indeed a success. Almost any Englishman will tell you this and therefore it is so.

The successful British executive reflects on these facts with a pitying smile for his symbol-minded American cousin as he leaves his club and settles himself on the caressing cushions (the leather comes only from the hides of *contented* cows) of his chauffeur-driven Rolls-Royce.

It is a fact widely recognized in Britain that a yearning for a big, air-conditioned, finny Cadillac is a manifestation of a basic insecurity which needs to be relieved by ownership of showy possessions, whereas the desire for a big, air-conditioned, *non*-finny Rolls-Royce is merely the natural desire for a well-made piece of machinery.

This is one of those differences between the peoples on the two sides of the Atlantic that are not easy to explain.

The Rolls-Royce may cost $20,000. It may have eighteen coats of paint, each hand-applied by a card-carrying member of the Royal Academy. The inside of the exhaust pipe may have been polished to mirror brightness by having trained minks run up and down it in emery-cloth slippers. But the Rolls-Royce is no man's vulgar success symbol. Englishmen have no need of external props. In any event, success symbols have fins—and the Rolls-Royce (perish the thought) has no fins.

Very many of the Rolls's one sees—and one sees very many if one is the sort who keeps an envious eye out for such things—are not owned by the people who are glimpsed in the back of them, lurking behind their *Times's*. Taxes being what they are, there aren't that many people able to pony up five thousand to eight thousand

122

quid to avoid riding the Tube and being breathed on by the Lower Classes.

Many of the Rolls's are company cars. Thus the managing director will get a Rolls, and lesser geniuses Daimlers, Austin Princesses, Jaguars, Rovers and so on, in strict order of their descending importance in the firm.

Again, this in no way attaches social significance to the automobile; such an interpretation is a purely North American failing. It is only a case of providing transportation suitable to a man's needs and station.

There is not in Britain, either, that feeling of its being necessary to have absolutely the most expensive car one can afford—or not afford—in order not to be despised by the neighbours. Take, for instance, the case of the Bentley, which Rolls-Royce frankly supplies for people who may be diffident about buying a Rolls. These are people who could afford a Rolls (or rate a Rolls with the firm) and who, by driving a Bentley, proclaim that they can (or do), but prefer to have this understood rather than stated. It is on such things as this that the British reputation for modesty and shrinking from ostentation is founded.

It is shrinking from ostentation, of course, which makes it unthinkable that any Briton should drive a car with, say, a raccoon tail on the radio aerial, or flaunt some other showy device of the sort for which North American juveniles of all ages have a lamentable weakness.

At most, the driver who goes in for "foreign touring"—a term which means he has been at least once across the Channel—may have a few badges. An accessory which may be bought here is a badge-bar, which stretches across the front of the car above the license plate.

There is no connection at all with what used to be called "line-shooting," or anything of that sort, if the badge-bar proclaims the owner's membership in the Automobile Association; the Royal Automobile Club; the Sports Car Club; the driving, touring or motoring clubs of France, Belgium, Luxembourg, Monaco and Lebanon; a regiment or regimental association; and with these, the crest of his city. Nothing ostentatious in that, goodness knows, and very helpful too, the Lebanese Motoring Club badge, if one should run out of petrol, say, on the road to Damascus. Bad road, that.

Preservation of the old term "motor touring" points to another

123

way in which the British attitude toward the automobile is different. The automobile continues to have sporting connotations. One naturally dresses for serious automobiling—tweed cap, muffler, sports jacket and driving gloves. (Goggles have largely disappeared.)

The sporting connection is revealed, too, in the terminology used by manufacturers. Instead of the simple, readily-understandable terms with which North Americans are familiar—*turbo-torque, multi-flow, coaxial down-draft shafts* and the like—U.K. manufacturers tend to employ sportier and more technical-sounding terms as *cc's, litres, gear-box ratios, twin overhead cams,* and *aspect ratios* (or is that airplanes?). And the British driver has a thorough grasp of the meaning of those terms which he uses so glibly—the same thorough grasp that his counterpart has of the *turbo-torque, multi-flow, coaxial down-draft shaft.*

The chronicle of a spartan
or, how I got my rowing blue

Saturday was the day of the Boat Race. Cambridge won. Oxford lost. Me too.

That was the 104th Boat Race and, having missed the first 103, it seemed none too soon to start catching up. Among the spectacularly bad ideas of our time, that one surely would come in the first twenty.

The following, allowing for a few places where my notes become blurred and unintelligible, is a fairly accurate chronicle of the day:

Awakened by young son crying, "Hey, Dad, it's snowing." Lecture young son on necessity of telling the truth, or at least coming closer to it than to suggest it's snowing in London in April. This is the time of daffodils.

7:37 Chill fear beginning to seep in, grope to window and come reeling back, snowblind. Consider apologizing to child, but instead lecture him severely on being a gloom-peddler and a blabber-mouth.

10:00 Snow having turned to rain, hopefully telephone a sportswriter to ask if race cancelled. No such luck. Ask where would be best place to see it. Hang up abruptly when he says: "Have you got a television set?"

124

11:50 Waterloo Station. Public address system playing "In the Mood." Answer, "No." Board train for Mortlake. *There's* a cheery name for a cold wet foggy day (had I mentioned it was now foggy?) "lake" as in "water," and "mort" as in "drop mort with pneumonia."

12:20 p.m. Mortlake. Raining harder than ever. Fog thicker than ever. Can see hand in front of face, but have to be standing close to it. Squelch off toward river, "just a step down the road," according to one of the natives, all of whom are congenital liars when it comes to distance. Three miles if it's a foot.

12:30 Meet swan on way. Is he on road, or am I in river? Does it matter?

12:32 Arrive at The Ship, riverside pub. Man on doorstep is telling son: "That post there is the finish line." Leaving son to marvel over this bit of intelligence, man nips into pub for a fast one. Nip in after him.

Half-pint of best bitter and two sausage rolls. Second half-pint of best bitter to see if it will loosen grease from sausage rolls congealed on roof of mouth. Pair of soggy doggies, those were.

Outside again. Someone has hung a sheet over whole of far side of river. Fog. Usually when you get rain and fog you get them separately, but not here. Here they've been practising with foul weather for centuries and can serve it up in all combinations.

And cold? Every man is going to get his rowing Blue today. He's also going to get his rowing goosepimples and rowing chilblains.

"Daddy, were you a rowing Blue at Oxford?"

"Blue? I was numb clear through."

1:00 (approx.) So murky a police boat going upriver has its running lights on. A Viscount whistles overhead looking for London Airport. The pilot probably has his hand out, feeling for the tops of buildings. A seagull goes by on foot.

1:10 Take up position with back to wall of a brewery. Sign above ("We Want Watneys") helps to sluice rainwater down back of neck. Woollen scarf soaked through. Shoes filled with water. Note-taking abandoned, pen guaranteed to write in bathtub having given up.

1:20 Squadron of swans in line astern come upriver on radar. Sealed bottle floats by near shore. Probably contains a note: "We are lost—Oxford."

St. John Ambulance crew goes by. What are they going to treat today—exposure cases? Approaching 1:30 starting time, fog begins to lift slightly, but rain intensifies.

125

1:30 Someone shouts, "They're off!" That means that four miles and a bit downriver at Putney Bridge the two crews are off. Hope that's what it means.

Cambridge half-length in front. Cambridge length in front . . . two lengths in front . . . six lengths in front. Take Oxford colours off lapel and put in inner pocket. Put up Cambridge colours.

Course follows great loop in river. If Oxford cox has head screwed on right, could steer across fields today— they're wet enough —and nip Cambridge. But he doesn't. Sneer at Oxford cox.

Radio says Cambridge has swept under Barnes Bridge four lengths in front. Haven't seen a thing yet; could have stood in cold shower at home and saved trainfare.

Through the mist, first glimpse of Cambridge crew, eight men bending, reaching, digging oar, little man at back bailing out rain water. Sorry; little man at back not bailing rain water. That's cox leaning forward and back as he calls stroke.

Oxford, well behind, seems to be stepping up stroke. No hope now of catching Cambridge. Maybe just trying to ward off pneumonia, or blue-mould. Race over. Little man selling ribbons now yelling, "Wear the winning colours." Is that the spirit that won at Waterloo?

Squelch back to railway station, back to Waterloo, into cab, arrive home, strip off soaked-through raincoat (made of cloth used by Sir Edmund Hillary in Everest expedition; can only say he's lucky it didn't rain), soaked-through scarf, soaked-through jacket, sweater, shirt, undershirt.

Hop into hot tub. Propel two of young son's boats down tub with big toes. Oxford wins. Nuts to Boat Race.

With flannels and blazer through darkest Henley

On the 9:48 a.m. from Paddington there was a fat young man in glasses, wearing a straw boater with a brown, blue and maroon band, a bottle-green blazer stretched to the point of peril across his broad beam, a pair of cream flannels also giving their utmost, and brown suede shoes. The blazer had brass buttons, and his tie matched the hatband.

Billy Bunter, the Fat Frump of the Fifth to a T. It was a disappointment not to find him scoffing cream buns out of a wicker hamper labelled "Tuck." But, perhaps like Bunter, he was counting on making off with his friends' provender once he got to Henley.

On the same train there was another Greyfriars man. (It was Greyfriars, wasn't it? Greystoke was the family name of Tarzan of the Apes.) This one was a more stalwart type, who would be called Jim, and who would have been captain of the School XI. He must also have been in the boat club. He was dressed for a day on the river in a blue blazer with crossed sculls on the breast pocket; a cream boating cap, which is like a cricket cap with slightly more peak; and cream flannels. He was perfectly the old schoolboy, an erstwhile straight bat and strong oar, an all-rounder, now, at thirty-eight or thirty-nine, becoming simply all rounder.

Bunter and Jim and I (brown jacket, grey slacks, hatless) changed at Twyford to another diesel-electric train. It took us past country stations where the station-masters had had time between trains to cultivate rosebeds, and through gentle woods and soft fields to Henley-on-Thames. Henley is the end of that particular line.

It's a mellow old town with a lot of that peculiarly English red brick that contains a lot of blue. There are some timbered buildings which may or may not be the real thing, and a parish church built entirely of small bricks chipped out of the native flint. The church, which isn't particularly old as things go here, has a squat tower with a blue-faced clock two-thirds of the way up.

Henley has an abundance of tea-rooms (including an improbable Ye Olde Elizabethan Tea Shoppe), and even more pubs. There's The Angel, and The Red Lion, The Carpenter's Arms, The Old White Hart, and, a less familiar name, The Catherine Wheel, among dozens of others.

The town library, at the other end of the street from the church, was decked with flags, including the United Nations flag, and many of the shops had put up pennants for Royal Regatta week.

By the time your correspondent (a budding Bunter himself) had scouted the tea shoppe situation, had had his coffee and two cakes, and had got to the river, Billy Bunter and Jim had been absorbed in a throng of Bunters and Jims.

The Englishman at play, as the Englishman at work, is happy

127

only when properly uniformed. Thus, a job in the City demands a bowler hat and invites striped pants; a countryman wears tweeds and never carries an umbrella; the youngest child goes to school in a blazer and peanut scoop hat; white flannels and a white cable-stitch sweater are essential to even a scratch game of cricket on the village green; and all the right people go to Ascot only in morning clothes. Suede shoes are worn to the pub for a Sunday morning pint.

The prescribed dress for Henley satisfies both the yearning for uniform and the native inclination toward the display of autobiographical symbols (the old school or regimental tie, the club crest, the automobile badge). The result at Henley is something beside which the North American beach shirt—an object of lofty amusement here—is as quietly decorous as a christening robe.

The Henley Royal Regatta may well be the world's most pleasant sports event. The course is a long, dead-straight stretch of the river, which flows oilily, the colour of a wine bottle, in the shadow of the dripping willows, the poplars and elms. Looking the length of the course toward the start, there are green hills for a backdrop, and on either side, fields as tame as lawns.

The stands and tents of the Henley Royal Regatta are on the Berks side of the river; across the way, on the Bucks side, there are the awninged stands of the Phyllis Court Club, an organization which a Henley official said coldly "has nothing to do with us." The club's stand, nevertheless, looks as if it has been there as long as the regatta has been going, which is since 1839.

Oxford University Boat Club beat Yale University by a handy two lengths in the semi-final of the Grand Challenge Cup—known to the initiate simply as the Grand—thereby guaranteeing an all-English final in the Eights for the first time in years. The effect on business in the several blue-and-white-striped bar tents was magical.

A young Australian, Stuart Mackenzie, two axe-handles wide across the shoulders, won easily ("easily" was the judges' verdict; it looked like five or six lengths) in the semi-final of the Diamond Sculls. He beat S. C. Rand.

An Australian voice in the press box said, "Atta boy, Stu," as Mackenzie swept by underneath, and Mackenzie, who later went on to win the Diamonds for the fourth year in a row, winked and smiled. He was breathing as easily as if he had been for a walk around the block.

At Henley, the boat-racing is really only an excuse for a lot of other things, such as hundreds of pretty girls standing around looking

128

pretty in petal hats and summer frocks, and people drinking gin-and-tonic under umbrellas, and old oarsmen getting themselves up in costumes that would agitate a colour-blind bat.

Billy Bunter and Resolute Jim, who had seemed exotic birds on the morning train, turned out to have been drab by comparison with most of their fellows. There was, for instance, the Old Something-or-Other in a blazer the colour of a cherry soda, with inch-wide royal blue braid around the lapels and pockets, and a white hat. And there was an Old Something-Else in a scarlet blazer with gold braid-ing, and an Old Whatever-It-May-Be in a dark green blazer, a salmon pink tie, and a huge pink carnation.

The band of the Life Guards whomped away at a military med-ley called "Pageantry." An old Oxonion told an acquaintance ". . . at Magdalen" (pronounced "Maudlin") "we won the Grand in '20-'21; I was in the second eight, actually."

The boatmen crowded into the Boatmen's Amenities Tent for lunch, and the pretty girls and the superannuated Billy Bunters and Resolute Jims revolved on the lawns. Down by the river, the loud-speaker hung in the trees announced the start of the next race, be-tween Eton and Shrewsbury.

Once could be a mistake but a second time is madness

Along with the Derby, the Ascot Gold Cup, Wimbledon, Henley, the Cup Final and whatever they do in midsummer at Lords, the Boat Race is one of the great sports events of the year in England.

There are several ways of seeing it. The easy way is in front of a television set. The wet way has already been narrated. The pleasant way on a good day is on the river bank, preferably just outside a pub. Another way is with wife, small son, five-month-old dachshund, car and picnic lunch. This way madness lies. Herewith a short chron-icle.

1:00 p.m. GMT. Arrive at Duke's Meadows, great grassy space on Middlesex bank, supervised for day by National Car Parks (ad-mission seven shillings and sixpence). Dog making loud sounds of

129

distress suggesting incipient car sickness. Release leg bolts from dog, child, put both out to grass.

1:01 Son returns. "I want a Coke."

Old man: "They don't have Cokes here."

Son: "They have ice-cream cones."

Old man: "But you said you wanted. . . ."

Son: "A double vanilla; that's a big one."

1:30 Over lunch, resident expert on Boat Race explains why Cambridge going to win. "Oxford had a revolt in the crew early in the year. There was talk about setting up a rebel crew. Some of last year's people aren't back. . . ."

Son: "Oxford is going to win."

Resident expert (indulgently): "Well, everyone to his own opinion; that's what makes the race, but. . . ."

Son: "Oxford will win easy."

1:45 Small son, surveying river traffic, announces: "There's a police boat."

Old man: "Yes? How do you know?"

Son: "It's black. If it was red it would be a fire boat."

2:00 Again studying river traffic, same authority spots dilapidated launch, a ragged hole in its side just above the water line. Says: "Boy! There's a wreckedy one."

Female parent: "Yes, isn't it? They'd only be able to use that one at low tide."

Male parent bangs head against nearby tree trunk.

2:15 Resident expert on Boat Races explains that this race has been going on for more than a hundred years.

Son: "Boy! How old are they?"

Old man: "Not very . . . . No, no; not the same people for a hundred years."

2:30 Small son chooses to explore shoreline at moment when a large launch sends in an appropriately large wash.

Parent: "Come back from th . . . . Did you get wet?"

Son: "Not much. Just my feet."

3:15 Race begins (about three miles away, at Putney).

Son: "Can I get on the car roof?"

Boost child onto car roof, thick with greasy film of winter's smogs. Female parent rolls eyes to heavens. Remove child, put car floor-mat on car roof, replace child.

3:25 Boats slicing up Thames, Oxford well in front. Child, face down on car roof, feet toward river, finds absorbing interest in trying to reach trunk lid.

3:35 Oxford wins by six lengths.

3:36 Child says: "You said Cambridge was going to win."

Male parent: "Yes, but. . . ."

Child: "But they didn't, did they?"

4:10 Traffic jam.

4:30 Dog making loud sounds of distress, suggesting incipient car sickness. Give dog sharp cuff about the lug. Give son one of same on principle. Snarl at wife.

I*gloo-lai-gar-djong-moo-lee-an-gee-tai-nar-po-geek**

For reasons which are not entirely clear to me, I seem to have stored away rather a lot of disjointed notes about Eskimos. You hardly ever get a call these days for the recipe for seals' bare feet, but here it is, large as life, along with some scribbled comments which are recognizable at twenty feet as being in one's own round hand:

"Seals' bare feet (seal flippers). Put the seals' bare feet in a cooking pan. Cover them with blubber and keep in a hot place until the fur comes off. Then it is time to eat the seals' bare feet. You can cook them or eat them without cooking."

If you are really hungry (says a scribble under this recipe), you don't even need to bother taking them off the seal. In this case it is only proper to allow the seal a bite of your own feet first, and then you can alternate. This is known (at least among Eskimos with a bit of the Irish in them) as "sealing one's own fate."

It's the risk of coming upon things like that and not knowing how to explain them, that causes newspapermen never, except on pain of excommunication, to delve into the files which they so laboriously keep. For instance, what would have motivated anyone to keep a note on family allowances (obviously the product of some department of government) for Eskimos?

* Neither one of us has ever gone to Chesterfield Inlet.

But there it is, lurking under the heading *Minakahimatit*—and goodness knows what *that* means.

Ikayugekklalaea-hugit anga-yukkar nutagainnik patigeekeplugit hakugikeplugitle, nunat Ataningita tatkhekhein taman minaetikaktait khetennganum Canadami nutakkamik humingaikhimatikhat pibluge; tamna tagitilik minak-himatik khetennganum.

So there you have it, and welcome to it. (All references in the foregoing text to amounts of $5 a month should now be amended to read $6, thanks to Walter Gordon, mighty hunter.)

Then how many people know what Eskimos call snow? (But for another fortunate note which says that Eskimos have no swear words, one might have leapt to the conclusion that Eskimos, who see so d--- much of it, might call it ----- or even ------. But they don't.)

For reasons now lost to history, the National Research Council one August—August, mind you—got up a little press release in which it undertook to inform the Canadian people about some score of scientific and Eskimo terms for snow.

The Eskimo terms won hands down. Somehow, *mang-uk-tuk* sounds like "snow that is getting soft." (He: "I put on my galoshes to walk in the mang-uk-tuk." She: "I certainly hope you didn't bring any of it in the house with you.")

Spatial dendrites and *graupel,* on the other hand—a couple of terms used by the civil savants of the Research Council—sound like the names of tools a dentist would use on your teeth. ("I've got rather a problem here, nurse; hand me the graupel.")

The council's approach to the whole stupefying subject was hesitant and almost apologetic, as it had every reason to be. It titled its discourse, "Snow Is Not Simple." The first sentence said, "Snow seems simple to many of us, but it is not—not if you get interested in it."

Thus having given the obvious answer—don't get interested in it—the council edged on: "The two kinds of people in Canada who appear to be most interested are the Eskimos and the scientists of the National Research Council. Perhaps the earliest system for classifying different kinds of snow was evolved by the Eskimos, who built it into their language. They have about twenty different names for aspects of snow that are most important to them."

What the council might have observed, but didn't, was that if the Eskimos hadn't built some score of terms for snow into their language they would have been severely handicapped for conversation

132

on those long winter nights. You can't talk about seals and whales forever.

Anyway, the council went on to say that some of the terms were *ah-put,* meaning snow in general; *ki-lu-kak,* soft snow; *i-ya-go-vak-juak,* snow crystals; *sa-ki-tu-vuk,* snow falling straight down; *ku-ah-li-vuk,* snow freezing as it falls.

Soft snow falling straight down and freezing as it falls? In such a situation it would be simpler to go into the igloo (*i-glu-vi-gak*) and stay there until either it (a) melted and went away, or (b) piled up, in which case it could be referred to simply as *mau-yak,* or soft, deep snow.

Water made from snow?—*i-mu-gak.* Snow like salt?—*pu-kak.* Snow for snow house?—*i-glu-sak.* Snow for banking house?—*kag-mak-sak.*

The National Research Council didn't make it clear whether "snow for banking house" meant snow for shovelling against the side of the house, or snow for a banking house like the Toronto-Dominion, or the Royal, or the Imperial Bank of Commerce. It very well may not be important.

The Eskimos also had a word for holes made in the snow by wind—*i-mek-ti-vi-ytu.* They do not appear to have a word for the sort of holes in the snow that people's eyes are sometimes described as looking like.

How to get down from a duck, *eider you know or you don't*

If you have been fretting about not knowing how to gather the down from the nest of the eider duck, you have come to the right place. Thanks to the Department of Northern Affairs and National Resources, which is a regular mine of information on matters pertaining to eider ducks, we have on hand what amounts to a do-it-yourself handbook on feather gathering.

First you go to the rocky offshore islands and coastlines of the Eastern Canadian Arctic. (Flights leave on the hour.) That's where the ducks are.

It is left to the individual to decide what he will gather his down in, but we should think that something between the size of a thimble and a demi-tasse, since the average nest (or duck, assuming single-owner occupancy) yields only half-an-ounce of down each year. It would depend to a degree on how energetic one was. In any case, it would seem unwise to start out with a pillowcase, because long Arctic days or no long Arctic days, there is a physical limit to the number of nests one can strip. You might as well face it.

So much for the harsher facts of eider down gathering. Now for the process itself. According to the Department, the down is normally collected about two weeks after incubation begins. The eggs are removed and placed carefully at the side of the nest. (Presumably the duck has been removed, or has removed itself, before this. If it hasn't, place the duck at the side of the nest, too.) Nearly all the down is taken out, except for a small pad which is placed in the bottom of the nest. The eggs (and duck, where applicable) are then replaced, resting on the small pad.

Is that clear? Up duck, eggs to one side, remove down, small pad in position, replace eggs, down duck. A second collection of down is usually made after the young leave the nest. This is known as the installment system—so much down down and the rest later.

The gatherer may be assured that the collection of down does not interfere with the hatching of the eggs. Northern Affairs does say, however, that "adult ducks may show some nervous reaction." What sort of reaction this may be—hives, twitching of the eyelids, post-nasal drip, psychosomatic colds—the Department does not say. But it is sympathetic: "Improved techniques of collection may result from the biologist's studies."

(One idea might be to train a squad of pickpockets who would gather the down right out from under the ducks without their ever knowing, a sort of Fagan's Furtive Fevver Finders.)

The biologist referred to was a chap who was going to spend the summer on Baffin Island "studying the lives, loves and mating habits of the eider duck." These were studies obviously to be undertaken discreetly. With creatures of such sensitiveness that they suffer nervous reactions from having their nests housecleaned, the effect of someone's prying into their love life might be shattering.

First thing you know, you could have a lot of ducks thinking that this everlasting moulting, moulting, moulting was doing nothing except provide quilts for man's back. Get a lot of eider ducks suffer-

134

ing from a quilt complex, and where's the eider down industry then, heh?

It gives you something to think about.

More about the endearing ways
of eider ducks (and Govs.-Gen.)

ITEM: Department of Northern Affairs and National Resources has announced that Eskimos at Frobisher Bay have presented the Governor-General with an eider down vest, dark blue with ivory buttons.

A question one ponders is whether,
At functions in inclement weather,
When the Viceregal chest
Might be clad in this vest,
Could His Ex then be said in full feather?

No doubt, somewhere in the frozen North, there is now a proud eider duck strutting around with his bald little chest stuck out, the the envy of every other duck for miles around.

Said a chap to the proud donor duck,
"To what do you credit your luck?"
Said the duck, "Goodness knows,
But one must, I suppose,
Assume that I showed lots of pluck."

The great beaver agreement
or, we really did give a dam

An idea that diplomats assiduously strive to foster among non-diplomats is that diplomats spend most of their waking hours saving the world from imminent disaster and wrestling with problems of so recondite a nature as to be not worth mentioning to laymen.

So much for diplomatic image-making. It happens that there has fallen into profane hands—in a word, mine—a small file of diplomatic correspondence about, of all mundane things, beavers. The contents of this file led in time to a small but dignified ceremony, celebrated with appropriate national honours, in Washington.

CANADA ONE (the offer): "After reading the interesting feature in the *Washington Post* about your hopes for re-creating a Beaver Valley, I wired my government in Ottawa to see if there were any spare beavers available in Canada.

"I find that there are surplus beavers available, right from Canada's capital, and that these could be provided for you any time you are ready. . . ."

UNITED STATES ONE (the gracious acceptance): "The National Zoological Park has had many years of pleasant contacts with various Canadian zoos, but it seems to me most appropriate that the beavers you mention should come from your capital city to ours. . . . The work on Beaver Valley has begun."

CANADA TWO (confirmation): "I am delighted to hear that Beaver Valley has begun and that it will be ready to welcome beavers from Canada in late spring or summer. . . . Perhaps you might give me an idea of the number of beavers required to start a colony."

UNITED STATES TWO (requisition, detail): "Theoretically, we could start a colony with a pair of beavers; three, one male and two females, would be better; if it is not too much to ask for, five, two males and three females, should fairly well insure the success of our project."

UNITED STATES THREE (dawning realization of complications): "I have been reading up on the life habits of beavers and find that they are strictly monogamous; that is, the males do not want other males around, and the females will whip out extra females.

136

"I therefore think that we had better request only one pair of beavers at a time, or perhaps two pair at most. The more I read of beavers, the more I wonder if we can actually make them build the dam where we want it. As you undoubtedly know, the beaver has a very determined mind of his own."

CANADA THREE (application of salve): "It was Ottawa who first suggested that we should provide three beavers. The Foreign Service officer who passed the word on suggested that it was hard to tell the sexes apart and that the third beaver was just a bit of insurance. . . .

"If the beavers act in Washington as they have sometimes acted in Ottawa, we will probably have new international difficulties which may succeed in diverting attention from some of the older problems we have shared."

CANADA FOUR (sex life of beavers, amplification): "The shipping of three or six animals is recommended because of the difficulty of ensuring the selection of a family group and avoiding the likely possibility of sending two bachelors with little incentive for a joint home-building programme. . . .

"If the monogamous nature of the American species is shared by the *Castor canadensis,* the problem of a successful selection of a pair appears to be complicated by the necessity of choosing not simply a mate, but rather the right one. No doubt wildlife experts [Ed. Note: Not to mention beavers] have overcome such obstacles in the past.

"The last problem raised—construction of a dam on the desired location—appears to present a test of man's mental superiority over the beaver. Since the beavers build dams for practical purposes, it would seem to be a challenge to the zoo attendants to arrange things in such a way as to make the spot they have in mind for the beaver the one the beaver would be most likely to select."

INTERNAL MEMORANDUM (Canadian): "Sex seems to be a complicating factor in our dealings with the zoological division of the Smithsonian Institution."

UNITED STATES FOUR (research continued): "In checking back in our records, when we established our first beaver colony a statement appeared in our annual report which I think is worth quoting: 'The beavers of the park are kept in two enclosures and in both of these have built themselves dams and shelters. It is found, however, that care must be taken to select them from a single family, as other-

137

wise they fight viciously. Four beavers died during the year from wounds received from their companions. . . .

"As a result of our 1896 experience, we had probably better not count on having more than one male and one female. . . ."

INTERNAL MEMORANDUM (Canadian): "You will note with relief that when the Ottawa beavers arrive in Washington they are going to live a life of moral rectitude. . . ."

Then, with the attendance of appropriate high dignitaries of the Canadian parliament, this international transaction was completed. Committed into the care of the zoological division of the Smithsonian Institution, as personified by Dr. A. Remington Kellogg, the assistant secretary, were three Canadian beavers.

Turned out that all that worry about getting two bachelors was wasted. The two didn't even wait for the formal presentation to produce a third.

If you're man's best friend
why do they treat me this way?

Among the things that are impossible, one is to take a boy out to look at pups with the thought that maybe you will buy one. You can go out to buy a pup, or you can stay home, but there is no in between, no "maybe."

There had been some talk among two-thirds of the people at our place about maybe buying a Boxer—talk which was kept quiet from the other one-third, which was firmly of the view that when you've seen one Boxer, you've seen 'em all. And she'd seen one.

So on a Saturday, the two-thirds went out to a place in Maryland to look, just out of curiosity, no more, at some offspring of Ch. Marquam Hill's Hurricane. The puppies, they had heard, were looking for people.

After just looking for a while, the one said, "What do you think?" and the other said, "I think we ought to get that one."

"That one" turned out to be called by the breeder, who had not formally named them yet, "George." George was a golden brindle with white on his chest and part of his mask, and with four white feet. The feet were of a size to ensure that he would not blow over in a high wind, and obviously he had a lot of growing to do to catch up with them.

So George, shortly to be renamed Blitz, was added to a household which already included a miniature dachshund named Willi. But first, when the two-thirds got home, they were met at the door by the unconsulted one-third who said:

"Where did you get that?"

"We just bought him."

"You can't mean it. But if you do, I'm leaving."

Apart from that she took it like a regular brick, with hardly a word except:

"All right. But don't expect me to look after it. You two must be out of your minds. We've already got one dog around here, jumping all over the furniture and shedding hair everywhere. It's all very well for the two of you. But who's going to feed them and take them out? And how are these two dogs going to get on, especially when that one gets bigger? And another thing. . . ."

And so on, for not a minute over an hour-and-a-half. However, she was eventually pacified with the solemn assurance that the newcomer wouldn't give a moment's trouble; that he was good natured, well mannered and intelligent, and would be fully trained in a matter of days.

The next day he climbed up into an upholstered chair and chewed the end out of one of the arms.

"They sometimes do things like that," said the senior resident dog expert. "He's probably teething."

"If he does anything like that again," said the lady of the house, "he isn't going to have any head to have teeth in."

Subsequently, in short order, he chewed the binding off the living room rug, gnawed the top edge of the lower portion of a Dutch door, knocked down and broke a lamp by becoming entangled in the cord, tore a cushion apart and scattered the filling through three rooms, substantially devoured the dachshund's basket, and showed a sturdy disinclination to have anything to do with the rules of hygiene which had been laid down for his guidance.

"Well," said the dog expert, "we can always tell people our dog is house-broken; he won't go anywhere but in the house."

"Very funny," said his mate.

So the expert got down the dog book which had enabled him to

139

teach the previous Boxer absolutely nothing, and he re-read portions of it. It contained the customary advice:

"Take the dog out immediately he has been fed, and before bedtime. Stay with him. Be patient. When he has done what he was brought out for, pat him and make a fuss over him. Soon he will come to associate praise with the act, and your troubles will be over."

In a manner of speaking, it worked. Then they had only to work out a way to break him of wetting the rug every time anyone patted him on the head.

Eventually it was decided that the thing to do, because he remained a high security risk at nights, was to lock him in the hall closet where, if suffocation didn't overtake him first, good manners possibly would (and perhaps vice versa). That did it. He would reel out of there in the morning, gasping on the fringes of asphyxiation, and go gratefully to the lane.

The Humane Society may not think much of the method, but to hell with the Humane Society.

And all the while, the lady of the house kept saying: "Sometimes I wonder about you. Have you forgotten what it was like with Schultz?"

Forgetting what it was like with Schultz would be an impossibility, short of taking a header out of a twelfth-floor window. Schultz had made a life work of making fools of people, notably his reputed master, and, while Schultz's successes in this undertaking were numerous, his greatest was in what came to be known as Schultz's Accident.

That was in Ottawa in January, on a night when the temperature was well below zero. Schultz was out, and when he had been out for about an hour there was a whining at the door. There he stood, on the step, cruelly crippled. His back was so badly humped that his back feet were up level with his front feet. He stood there dejectedly, hunched like that, as if he had dragged himself the last step that his poor strength allowed, and was now home only to die.

"My God," said his master, "he's been hit by a truck."

Whereupon he cradled the stricken creature in his arms and gently carried him, all sixty-five pounds of him, upstairs to a room where there was a spare couch. If Schultz was going to go, he was not going to go, alone, in the basement. He was bundled up with a blanket and hot-water bottle and left.

The next morning he was carried downstairs and into the car, carried into the veterinarian's office, and placed carefully on the examining table. He was gone over from top to toe. Eventually the vet said:

"There's not a thing I can see wrong with him. There are no broken bones; there don't even seem to be any bruises. Apart from his back, there are only those torn claws on his back feet . . . you see . . . as if he'd torn them trying to get a foothold on the ice or something?"

He paused. "You know what I think? I think he went out and found himself a girl friend and the cold got him in the back."

Then he said: "Shall I put him on the floor, or were you planning on carrying him out again, too?"

You can always show a dog but you can't show him much

Last fall, Blitz was at the vet's for some shots, when we got a call from a young woman who introduced herself as being on the staff there and said:

"Have you ever thought of showing your dog?"

"Have we ever thought of showing him what?"

"No, I mean putting him in a show. He's quite a nice puppy and there's a show coming up in Philadelphia on November 30th that would be just right for him."

She said that she was a handler and that if it was all right with us, she would go ahead and send in the entry form and, on the day, take him up to Philadelphia and show him.

We said, "No, thanks very much," as Blitz had been bought to scare off burglars and to perform other utilitarian tasks, such as giving the master of the house some exercise.

It was only later that dat ol' debbil curiosity got in. So what could it cost? Seven dollars for the entry fee, and a few dollars for the handler's fee. We phoned and said OK, go ahead.

She said her fee would be $20, and there would be some slight expense in getting the dogs to Philadelphia—she would be taking five or six—putting them up overnight and getting them back again. The expense would be shared equally among the several owners.

141

It was only later that the idea took hold that to have a dog in the dog show in Philadelphia without going to *see* him in the dog show would be foolish and possibly even cause for a reproach from the Humane Society. So it was decided that the two male members of the family would take a run up to Philadelphia on the appropriate weekend to have a look.

Since Philadelphia is no distance at all from Washington, it was decided that the car would be more trouble than it would be worth and they would go by train. Reservations were made by phone and when the tickets were picked up it turned out that they cost $34.

Obviously, with the judging to start on the Saturday morning, they would need to go up on the Friday night, which necessitated a hotel reservation. That Saturday was the Saturday of the Army-Navy game, which regularly attracts a crowd of a hundred thousand or more, and hotel space was at a premium.

In fact it was at such a premium that the only room which several telephone calls and wires could turn up was one at $24. But there was no turning back by then.

So they went up to Philadelphia and arrived just in time for dinner, which they had at Old Original Bookbinder's, a very good seafood house, where Christopher decided that just the ticket to assuage the pangs was a *crab imperial.*

The dinner cheque came to $8.

In the morning, when they came down for breakfast, the lobby was full of excitement of the big game and Christopher said, gee, he wished they were going.

And his pa said: "So do I. But there wouldn't be a chance. They get a hundred thousand people at that game and tickets are sold out months in advance."

"We could try."

"Sure, we could try, but I know what the answer would be."

So, full of assurance that it would be a gesture which couldn't possibly cost anything, an inquiry was made at the hall porter's desk. He said it was impossible, but to stop by on the way back from breakfast, anyway.

When they stopped by on the way back from breakfast the hall porter said:

"Here are your tickets. Seventeen-fifty. Eight-seventy-five apiece."

142

Christopher said: "Oh, boy, wait till the kids hear I was at the Army-Navy game."

The hall porter said: "You'll want tickets on the special bus that will be leaving from outside the hotel and bringing you right back here after the game. That will be four dollars for the two of you."

The third party didn't say anything.

They went out to the dog show, which proved to be a $1.50 cab-ride away, and bought a $1.25 catalogue-programme and had a thirty-five-cent hot dog and a twenty-cent bottle of pop each, and took another $1.50 cab-ride back to the hotel just in time to catch the bus to the football game where they had more hot dogs and pop.

Blitz took a third ribbon in his class, which wasn't bad, looked at one way. Looked at another way, however, it wasn't so good since there were only two other dogs in his class.

Blitz's share of the overnight expenses in Philadelphia turned out to be $19. It's only a mercy that he didn't have dinner at Old Original Bookbinder's, which, on second thought, he may have had.

Baa-baa black sheep
have you any explanation?

In Chicago, William E. Pepelko and Moses T. Clegg of the Department of Animal Husbandry, University of California, have told all about the ways of the male sheep. And a tawdry all it makes, too.

Their findings, if one may so dignify such tittle-tattle, were presented to a scientific session of the Federation of American Societies for Experimental Biology, in a paper titled: "Factors Affecting Recovery of Sex Drive in Sexually Exhausted Male Sheep."

There is no indication—there never is, scientists being the way they are—of what may have set two of them to studying a matter of such seemingly marginal interest (except perhaps to a few sheep). Squalid curiosity, perhaps. Or maudlin pity. Any day now someone in California will be getting up a Take-a-Sexually-Exhausted-Male-Sheep-Home-to-Lunch Week.

Whatever their motives, Messrs. Pepelko and Clegg began by

defining, to their own satisfaction at least, what constitutes a sexually exhausted male sheep. That's a sheep which (who?), for a period of twenty minutes or more, shows no interest in a sheep of the opposite biological persuasion.

This is bound to strike the layman as a peculiarly short length of time on which to base conclusions about a sheep's frame of mind. Twenty-minutes of standing around on three legs and whistling through his teeth, could equally well be attributed to confusion, astigmatism, or simple gentlemanly reticence.

Mr. Pepelko and Mr. Clegg obviously have a poor opinion of male sheep.

However, by a stroke of the purest good fortune, there has just come to hand the rough draft of a minor operatic work which, one would hope, would contribute to an understanding of the male sheep's problem—for such it is. As we begin, we find a clean-cut young male sheep singing "There'll Never Be Another Ewe."

> No matter when or where I am,
> You'll remain my little lamb,
> Baa-a-aby;
> How I love your fleecy charm,
> Keep yourself down on the farm
> So's your chops don't come to harm,
> Baa-a-aby.
>
> Frolic we midst Nature's gifts,
> Who live as wards of farmers,
> The race, I fear, is to the Swift's
> (Or maybe even Armour's).
>
> No matter what they say or do,
> It's ewe for me and me for ewe,
> Baa-a-aby;
> Affection we shall never stint,
> We two will stick like serge and lint
> Until they sprinkle us with mint,
> Baa-a-aby.
>
> Gambol gaily while we may,
> Let's have our fill of clover,
> For soon they'll. . . .

But that will give you the idea. This is a constant, devoted, unfickle ram we've got on our hands here, concerned only with thoughts of his one true love and the meat packer.

But wait. Hark! What is it that Pepelko and Clegg are saying to the Federation of American Societies for Experimental Biology out in Chicago?

Their studies, they are saying, point to the conclusion that "there is a reduction of sex drive associated with habituation to the same partner." Say it ain't so, Joe. *Et tu, Brute?* And all like that. Can it be? It can. Presently it becomes necessary to introduce a small plaintive chant by a small plaintive sheep (female). It is called "Habituation."

> We enjoyed a situation which began as fascination
> And with time and inclination grew until infatuation
> Was the one interpretation which in sober contemplation
> Any thinking sort of person could have put upon the case;
> In my state of great elation, not to say felicitation,
> There was nil anticipation, lacking any intimation,
> That a strange disinclination to prolong participation
> In this fond association even then was taking place;
> I beseech appreciation of my state of perturbation,
> Of my utter desolation, not to mention consternation,
> At his sudden declaration of impending termination
> Of our conjugal relation—I felt shattered and bereft;
> When I sought in desperation to promote a conversation
> Where by calm solicitation I would gain an explanation
> Which might serve as embrocation to my inner laceration
> He just baaaa-ed "Habituation"—and with that abruptly left.

Damn ram took it on the lam.

There's a possibility the chant will be found out of character with the tragic nature of the events portrayed, in which case a substitution can be made—of something along the tender lines of the song "Imagination" of some years ago.

> Habituation is lousy,
> It turns a sunny day frowzy,
> And makes a ram go all drowsy,
> Just as he. . . thinks of ewe;
> Habituation is chilling,
> Of ten-der-ness frequently killing,
> It makes a ram all unwilling
> Just as he. . . thinks of ewe. . . .

145

And so on.

But wait (again). Hark! What more are Messrs. Pepelko and Clegg saying? Nothing except that an old ram encountering a new ewe enjoys, if one may put it that way, a 95 per cent recovery of what seemingly are his normal interests—not to say obsessive preoccupations.

Well now:

> Said a ram to his mate, "Dear, in lieu
> Of some clinical sort of review
> Let me say, if I flit,
> It's been proved I'm more fit
> With a ewe that's not ewe but is newe."

It gives one something to think about, remembering, of course, that Pepelko and Clegg were talking about sheep.

Baa-a-a-a.

WASHINGTON

My life in the affluent society

Ready now? repeat after me:
I will not speak out plainly

Since I was moving to Washington, there did not seem to be any reason to anticipate difficulty language-wise (as we say), but then, how was anyone to know beforehand about the great U.S. love affair with the word "out."

Anyone who doubts that such a love affair exists can prove it for himself—pardon, can check it out—by soliciting help with some matter of public information almost anywhere in Washington. Helpfulness abounds, and the questioner can be sure that if the answer is not immediately at hand, someone will take hold of the inquiry—inquiries are always taken hold of—and will check it out. He may even be told that someone will "check it right on out," which is better still.

At the Pentagon, ever virile in word and deed, he may even come upon an official who will promise to "take hold of his question, and check it to hell-and-gone right on out," but experience shows that this sort of person rarely phones back.

If the questioner has offered some proposition of his own to be confirmed, he may find, after the process of checking it out has been completed, that it does not "prove out," or has not "proved out."

In politics it is exceedingly common—in fact, it is expected—that a candidate will say that he has had his opponent's programme "costed out," and found that it would be ruinously expensive. "Costed out" is a term that is intended to conjure up visions of electronic computers at work (clicketa-clicketa-clicketa) whereas in fact what it actually means is simply, "I had a couple of the boys in the back room add up the cost of his proposals to get a result favourable to us."

When a politician's platform or anything else has been costed out, the proper form of reporting the result is to say that it costs out at $6 million, or whatever the figures may be. The use of the simple "costs" is to be avoided as suggesting political amateurism.

Of course, if the politician whose programme is here involved were to cost it out himself, he would arrive at a much smaller figure. He would do that by separating out those expenditures which were of the nature of long term investment, from those which were irrecoverable. Having done this, he might be said to have "split out" certain expenditures, or to have "split them off" from certain others. An Adlai Stevenson might say simply that he separated these expenditures from those expenditures—but, of course, everyone knows what happened to Adlai Stevenson.

Not long ago, a Washington newspaper said that it doubted if the views of many voters would be changed "from here on out." This is the sort of thing that cannot be checked out with any certainty even by a Dr. George Gallup, and one can do nothing but wait until the ballots are counted—or even counted out—to see if the prediction proved out.

There, now, that's showing progress.

There are just one or two more simple rules to master. No one ever simply meets anyone, but "meets with." One says that something is "not too important," or "not too big," or "not too expensive" (having been costed out first, of course), or "not too common," and only rarely that it is unimportant, small, inexpensive, or rare.

One should strive to avoid the direct statement and to introduce colourful circumlocutions wherever possible. This, from a man who first promised to put some documents in the mail, makes a good example: "No, better than that, since I'll be coming down your way this afternoon, I'll hand-process them."

There are innumerable places where this term may be substituted for trite phrases; for instance, "Has the milkman hand-processed the milk yet?" Watch for your opportunities, and make the most of them.

It is wise always to keep an eye open—or an ear open, if you prefer—because the expression that will add colour to your speech may crop up anywhere. For instance, it was in one of his talk-derbies on television that David Susskind, the noted producer and interviewer, added a new gem to the language. He was talking with a Southern gentleman who was relating some of the practices used in his town to see that the races did not come into unwholesome proximity to one another. "Yes," Mr. Susskind expostulated, "but how does that stand Christian ethics-wise?"

It was a humble want-ad in the *Washington Daily News* which

150

added a new dimension to perfection (the detergent ads have been doing it for years, of course) in describing a used car. It was, said the ad, "immaculate in the extreme." This has a certain ring to it and should be kept in mind for use, for instance, by the housewife who has grown tired of describing her wash simply as "whiter than white."

Another colourful expression, "orbiting" continues to be popular. One speaks of government spending having "gone into orbit"—or one does if one belongs to the opposition party. It means that spending has increased, which is a less dramatic way of putting it and therefore to be avoided.

The uses to which "orbit" or "orbiting" can be put are limitless. For instance, the politician may want to use it in such a context as this, speaking of the plight of senior citizens (not old people), who live on fixed incomes: "They are caught in the squeeze of an inflationary spiral that has gone into orbit."

By George, you've got to admit it rolls off the tongue.

*P*lease, dear, would it be OK if I wrote about NAOERFMEDM?

As long as the mailman continues not to let snow, hail or the dark of night stay him from the swift completion of his appointed rounds, no denizen of the National Press Building is going to go short of diverting reading material with which to while away the hours.

Taking a lease on an office in the National Press Building is tantamount to signing up for a lifetime supply of mail so rich in nutty goodness as to be fattening, especially around the ears. Where else, for instance, would one go to hear from a Larston D. Farrar, founder of the National Association on Equal Rights for Men (Especially Divorced Men), or NAOERFMEDM, for short?

Mr. Farrar, who says at the outset that he is being sued in a district court for $2,000 in back alimony, defines the objectives of the new organization as being to "work for the restoration of male privileges and prerogatives and some simple justice in each of the states, except Virginia which is a hopeless case."

"The Old Dominion," says Mr. Farrar, "began to slide, from the

151

standpoint of male supremacy, when George Washington married for money."

The judge who awarded alimony to Mr. Farrar's former wife was a Virginia judge, a fact which ought not to be assumed to have affected Mr. Farrar's objectivity. Mr. Farrar has a low opinion of the chances of a man's getting justice in any court. The way he looks at it, the judge is likely to be married and "the judge's wife would bust him one if he ever gave a man a break in court."

It's something to think about, as is the prospect of becoming, for a trifling $1 a week, a member of the board of directors of Adventure Unincorporated (subject to the approval of the board, according to the letter) and be thereby entitled to join in the establishment of affiliated ventures and eligible to share equally in the divided profit therefrom.

If pressed, I might admit to not knowing what that means, but it has an aura to it like no other offer that has come this way since the last offer of the people behind the Warrenton Gold Cup to admit me as a sponsor for $15. The Warrenton Gold Cup people, whose business is running a fashionable steeplechase in the fashionable Virginia horse country, send out beautiful, engraved invitations, along with cards which say "I [accept / cannot accept] your invitation to become a sponsor of the Virginia Gold Cup Races," and even enclose prepaid reply envelopes.

They also bark up the occasional wrong tree, as one wrong tree is prepared to testify.

But this is getting away from Adventure Uninc., as it pleased to call itself. Its publication, *Ye the People,* explains what might appear to the lay eye to be a haphazard way of selecting people to join the board of directors:

"Commenting on this unusual criterion for picking directors, the spokesman thinks it compatible with the expressed aims of the company, when evaluated. He avers that the board positions must be filled by someone, and who is more apt to be the calibre person sought for leadership and trust than those who, quite evidently, are above average in vision, temperament and spirit. . . ?"

Correspondents are notoriously the calibre persons who are sought for positions of leadership and trust and the rest of it fairly describes this one to a T, but, it takes the edge off it, to have it so casually noted that the board positions have to be filled by *someone.*

An opportunity to join in giving leadership, without its even costing $1 a week, came from Alfred P. Adamo, of 11711 Oakland Avenue, Detroit, who was working up a crusade to see that Christopher Columbus got his due, which apparently he hasn't been getting these four-hundred-odd years. Under a picture of Columbus in long hair and a short skirt (his sailors may not have been uneasy only about his navigation), Mr. Adamo wrote: "We are all proud of John Glenn's pioneer venture into the unknown, with no charts or technicians to guide him. We honour John Glenn. Should we not also honour Columbus? His day, October 12th, is already a legal holiday in twenty-six states. Shall we not honour him in fifty states?"

Mr. Adamo's letter arrived in an envelope bearing the legend "Freedom and private enterprise have built cities, produced jobs, protected America, but socialism will deteriorate our country. Be Aware." That, of course, raised the pretty question of where Columbus would have been without a government handout in the form of Isabella's jewels.

The day that Joseph Plowsky, of 808 West Cuyler Avenue, Chicago, wants honoured is April 25, 1945, the day that United States soldiers met Russian soldiers at the Elbe and United States diplomats met Russian diplomats at San Francisco. He is the sponsor of San Francisco-Elbe River Day. It has not caught on.

There was also the congressman's office which put out a press release saying that the congressman had made a "dramatic and surprisingly frank plea" in behalf of a bill. If frankness on the part of the congressman is surprising to his own office, it will take no great effort to persuade *me* that it's not his long suit.

Those watercress sandwiches they'll get you every time

Diplomats are solemn, dignified men, who, according to the popular fancy, are given only (in the rare moments when they tear themselves away from their awesome tasks) to meditative walks in the country and cold baths.

Smash goes another illusion.

Solemn and dignified on the job they may be, but once out of the striped pants and into the dry martinis and they're regular devils. Or so one would gather from Washington landlords.

The State Department from time to time has had words with property management people, when seeking to insure that African diplomats will be able to find suitable housing—which is a polite way of saying that it occasionally has had to put the heat on landlords to quit discriminating against coloured people.

Or at least foreign-born coloured people.

Once, when one of these chats was going on, a number of landlords threw up their hands in horror and said that it wasn't African diplomats they didn't like. They just didn't like diplomats.

An untidy lot, apparently. One landlord complained that he'd had a diplomat tenant—colour unspecified—and had to scrub the place for weeks afterwards to get it clean. Another got into the press as the author of the remarkable statement: "We can't have diplomats. They entertain lavishly with caterers and orchestras until two in the morning."

A good question would be what sort of wild carryings-on even a diplomat could get up to with a caterer at two in the morning. Pelting one another with watercress sandwiches, perhaps? But whatever it is, landlords don't like it.

They also don't like diplomats because diplomats have diplomatic immunity—which means that they are hard to sue for the cigarette burns on the piano—and because they move house perpetually.

For myself, I have had a number of diplomatic friends and a nicer lot of people you'd be hard put to find. At least, of that type.

Run and give Daddy a hypo
Mummy's too busy to play now

Somewhere on Christmas morning a small boy, flushed from sleep and buzzing with excitement, comes tumbling down the stairs and in a moment exclaims, "Oooh, look, Mummy; just what I wanted. Santa has brought me a hypodermic needle for my very own."

(I think, as a Christmas present to myself, I'll have my head sent out and tested. I don't think I'm well. Not after frolicking among the kiddy things in the capital of the affluent society.)

For the jaded child who has simply everything, why not the Hypo-Phony? It's on sale in a Washington toy store, a life-size hypodermic, with graduated glass barrel, plunger, and needle two inches long, all so real that one father, whose trembling fingers have difficulty finding these typewriter keys, almost fainted dead away on the spot.

"Fakes hypo shots," the card said. "Pretend to give a shot to yourself, blood to an anaemic friend, hot blood to a cold girl, pep to a tired person."

Along with the needle, the imaginative parent will give the child an ordinary kitchen teaspoon, a small packet of white powder, a candle, and instructions on how to prepare himself a fix. Be a Dad to him; with your help he may be the first kid in the block on junk before he's ten. Anyway, it's better that he learn that sort of thing at home than pick it up in the streets.

Perhaps his interests lie in another direction. How about the Visible Woman Assembly Kit? If there's a manly little chap about your place who has been bugging jolly St. Nick for a build-it-yourself woman, this is for him.

The card propped up on top of the boxes said:
The Visible Woman
Assembly Kit
From Skin to Skeleton
Assemble, Remove,
Replace All Organs
$2.49

After he's had one of those, you're going to have trouble pushing those musty old yarns about the birds and the bees, but, by George, it will be worth it to see his beady little eyes light up on Christmas morning.

In the afternoon, when he tires of makebelieve, he can give Daddy a shot with the hypo and remove his gall bladder with the carving knife. ("Oh, dear, now look what you've done. And all over Mother's nice carpet. And Daddy's going to be angry, too, if he wakes up.")

Oh, and there are lots of other instructive toys that parents, bent on seeing their nippers grow up attuned to the world we live in, will want to keep an eye peeled for.

For instance, there's a car-train game. There are two true-to-scale cars which may be set to race at a true-to-scale 150 miles an hour, trying to beat a true-to-scale train to the level crossing.

Obviously sometimes—*ker-pow*—and then the kids can play doctor and nurse (with the Hypo-Phony) and insurance adjuster and things like that.

Or there's the homely, old-fashioned atomic cannon at $4.98. What child will not enjoy making just-pretend mushroom clouds? And it will give him a feeling for the real thing.

While the sprat is amusing himself rearranging the viscera of his Visible Woman and lobbing atomic shells onto the cat, his parents can relax, comfortable in the knowledge that they have done their best for him.

But, it was a woman at the Fort Meade army base, near Washington, who wrote her newspaper to say that there were some things regrettably missing among children's toys. Where, she asked, was a Russian roulette game, complete with paste-on hole-in-the-head, and the Junior Mugger Set, comprising mask, length of Venetian blind cord and a sockful of rocks?

Where, indeed?

While *below we're snugly sleeping*
Mother's up there staunchly beeping

Representative Victor Anfuso (D., N.Y.) is the brave man who opened his congressional subcommittee to hear representations from women who wanted to be allowed to follow men (as everywhere else) into space.

The children of the first spacewoman sing:

> She stood up her broom in the closet,
> She hung up her apron, and then
> With a wave to old Dad, she just rose from the pad
> And never was sighted again.

It's hardly a thing to be wondered,
We young ones are tearfully glum,
And we curse the day when, as she said, "Colonel Glenn,
Has nothing at all on you, Mum."

Still, we're proud she's our first astronautrix,
Though we pleaded with her that she stay,
But her systems were go, and she went, as you know,
And she beeps overhead to this day.

It seems that at about the time she was ready to make her re-entry, she found that her retro rockets wouldn't fire. So there she is in (beep, beep) perpetual orbit. It's hard lines, but you can't win 'em all.

Ah, once again 'tis spring the questing tourist quests

Once again the cherry blossoms are in bloom and the capital of the United States is in the grip of the hairy hordes from the outback. If there is one thing the natives of this country like to do when they've got a minute it's to run up to the national capital to genuflect in front of the monuments, living and dead. In this respect the place is totally unlike Ottawa, where no Canadian from anywhere else in the country would be seen dead, unless he'd been elected. (None of the tourists who turn up in Ottawa are Canadians, but are United States citizens who are on two-capitals-for-the-price-of-one tours. Ottawa is the other one.)

Canadians, when they set out to see a capital, come to Washington, where they traipse their children past the Federal Bureau of Investigation, the home of the United States' only living saint; the Justice Department, where Jack Paar's friend Bobby Kennedy works; and the Pentagon, the "big top" from which Steve Canyon takes his orders.

United States citizens, on the other hand, flock to their capital as if the House Unamerican Activities Committee would hold it against them if they didn't—which it undoubtedly would in any given case. Especially in the spring, they come down from the hills and up from the bayous and in from the plains to sniff the cherry blossoms, get rained on, torture their feet, and be awed. (The only tourist who was ever awed in Ottawa was one who dropped into one of the city's celebrated potholes and had to be rescued by a party of spelunkers.)

Where the tourists mostly torture their feet is in the line to get into the White House, where, once admitted, they jog-trot like har-

157

riers through the East, Green, Blue, and Red rooms and the State Dining Room. They go through so fast that a state dinner could be in progress and hardly any of them would notice.

In any case, they depart happy in the knowledge that they have spent a few moments under the same roof as the man down the hall who bears the Staggering Responsibility and the Awesome Burdens of the Most Powerful Office on Earth.

(Tourists are not admitted to 24 Sussex Street, but it may be that nobody has asked.)

In logical sequence, the tourists move next to the Capitol where, presiding over the House, they find the Man Who Exists a Heartbeat from the Presidency—Representative John W. McCormack. It's a sobering thought.

From there it is only a step down the hall to the chamber occupied by the United States Senate, the Greatest Deliberative Body in the World. Should a filibuster be going on about civil rights, the Senate is worth a visit if for nothing more than a look at one of the world's great collections of Petrified Attitudes. Beside them the Elgin Marbles in the British Museum are downright inconstant.

Tourists with some leisure and an interest in antiquities may spend some happy hours examining the machinery of government that is to be found at the Capitol. This machinery was contemporary with James Watt's steam engine, but, unlike the latter, has not been improved upon since. In 1964, this machinery made one of its notable achievements when it passed tax legislation, fifteen months after it was introduced, to ameliorate economic conditions which had been acute six months before that. The Congress of the United States is one of the last great strongholds against automation.

(Visitors to the Canadian parliament, if any, are somewhat compensated for the absence of so antique a legislative engine by the opportunity to see the Executive at work in the Legislature. "A mighty nice little parliament you've got up there," said Fred Ingleby, of Wichita, Kansas, after a recent visit. "Lyndon would have that place humming." Canadians generally agree—54 per cent, according to a recent survey, out of conviction, the other 46 per cent out of fear of seeming anti-American.)

Other fun places to visit in Washington are the State Department, at Foggy Bottom, and the Central Intelligence Agency, across the Potomac in Virginia. Neither of them admits visitors. That's what makes them fun.

Don't delay; book today.

158

That was the week that wasn't
or, sometimes life's like that

Wherein a languid correspondent reviews a weak week:

Monday: Dr. William W. Valletton, a leading ophthalmologist at the Medical College of South Carolina, reported that a glass of beer can improve a golfer's putting. It seems that a beer may increase convergence tone, whatever that is.

It wasn't clear from a news report whether the doctor was saying that the golfer should confine himself to one beer in order to reap this alleged benefit, or if he might allow himself one beer per hole—which could result in a lot of soggy golfers.

> My second shot was wildly off,
> It fetched a trap I hadn't seen,
> I sought my wedge to loft it up,
> At best, perhaps, I'd reach the green;
>
> But, wait, what's this the bag contains,
> What treasure greenly nestles here?
> Ahhh, succour for the duffer, this,
> That aid to keener vision, beer.*

(Denotes brief passage of time for consumption of beer.)

> The wedge goes back, what need of that?
> The putter now comes into play,
> The lines of sight run true, converge,
> (The cup's but eighty feet away);
>
> The clubhead strikes and follows through,
> The ball goes spurting forward, and
> A yard or so away it stops
> —He must have meant some other brand.

Tuesday: Oh, there are probably going to be people who won't believe this, but a pair of psychologists, Meller and Manian Breland, are busy training fish so that they (the fish, obviously) will behave as they did in their natural habitat when they are put into the new National Aquarium a few years hence.

---

* The properly appointed golf bag henceforth will provide—in addition to places for four woods, nine irons, spare shoes, balls, tees, pencil, and windbreaker—a refrigerated compartment equal to holding eighteen bottles of what will be known euphemistically as "Daddy's little helper."

159

A news report said: "If they were just dumped into their new habitat, practically nothing of public interest or scientific value would happen."

Undoubtedly true. Up to now, fish in aquaria have rarely shown a tendency to do anything but swim. Even at the zoo it has been left mainly to the monkeys to do anything of public interest and scientific value. (This occurs usually in the presence of some child—inevitably yours—who loudly wants to know now—no, not when he gets home—what they are doing.)

> Said the cod, "You can take it from me,
> When you've dwelt out of sight in the sea
> You're not lightly disposed
> To go on all exposed
> With whatever [he blushed] it may be."

Wednesday: Dr. John A. Freeman, of Duke University, a research associate in parapsychology (a branch of psychology which experiments in extra-sensory perception, among other things), said the Russians are doing military work in that occult field.

He told an audience in Greensboro, N.C., that the Russians believe that some day soldiers will be able to communicate with people in space ships without using radios.

> The astronauts's wife, having seen him embarked
> And shot off with a bellowing roar,
> Returned to the place where they'd recently parked,
> Where she stopped at their car, by the door.
>
> She thought a great thought to the man overhead,
> Which he heard with the utmost unease,
> For it seemed that the message was simply, "Drop dead,
> You've gone off and you've taken the keys."*

Thursday: In Potomac, Maryland, some people were taken into court by their neighbours because of their 150-pound Great Dane, Dana. Dana doesn't seem to have been vicious, but rather aggressively playful.

For instance, one of the neighbours complained bitterly that Dana kept leaping at his small sports car. It makes a pretty picture:

* The wife who hadn't taken the course in thought-transference would simply wait until he got back, when she would say in the time-honoured manner: "Oh, it's all right for you blasting off into space all the time, but what about me, tied down here? You might have a little consideration, etc., etc., etc."

He backed it out, he started off,
He gunned it for the open stretch,
He'd got a hundred yards or so,
When some misguided clod yelled "Fetch."

And there was good old Dana, bounding up the walk, the car
in her teeth and the driver frantically shifting down into second in
hope of a quick getaway if the wheels ever touched ground.

Friday: In Chicago, Dr. R. W. Bauer, director of the Department of Health Education of the American Medical Association,
said that men who call salads rabbit food ought to remember what
rabbit food does for rabbits.

"The male rabbit," he said, "is light on his feet, has no paunch
and maintains a lively romantic interest in lady rabbits."

That's all very well, but it doesn't seem to have occurred to the
doctor that there may be some of us who don't want to develop a
lively romantic interest in lady rabbits.

I greatly desire to be light on my feet,
And my paunch I'd do much to diminish,
So lettuce it is, if it's that I must eat
To improve my exterior finish;

But still I'd regard it a gain by no means,
If on ceasing from meat-eating habits,
I found as result of my living on greens
I'd developed an interest in rabbits.*

The KKK—out of the files and into their sheets

Tuscaloosa, Alabama

The Ku Klux Klan is something that anyone who was a kid in the
1920's probably lumps with bathtub gin, flappers, the stock market
crash—things of his time that he knows about only because of later
reading. And here was the Klan, the KKK, burning cross, hooded

---

* Playboy Club bunnies, of course, are a cottontail of another colour, as any red-blooded, meat-eating American boy knows.

men, secret symbols and all, straight from the old newspaper files, on a steaming hot night in Alabama in the 1960's.

The Klan met in a farmer's field a few miles outside of town and burned a forty-foot cross on a small rise of ground, because Vivian Malone and James Hood, who are Negroes, were asking to be admitted to the University of Alabama.

In other times, the fiery cross in the night sky would have caused all those whom the Klan hates—Negroes, Jews, Catholics, foreigners, but most particularly Negroes—to shiver in their beds. Not now.

Now, the Klan is a pinch-faced young man doing violence to the English language from the back of a flat-bed truck as he talks on and on in the hot night about the Communist conspiracy which makes the Negro its tool. Only a few of his hearers on the stubble field arouse themselves sufficiently to shout an occasional "Amen."

The young man is Robert Shelton, a tire salesman by day, who glories by night in the rites and titles of Imperial Wizard of the United Klans of America. Bobby Shelton is the national leader.

The Klan drew a good crowd that night. Cars were parked nose to tail, on both sides of the road and on the grass strip down the middle, for several hundred yards along the Route 11 bypass outside Tuscaloosa. Many more cars were parked in the field itself. The number of cars, in fact, seemed too great for the number of visible people, suggesting that at Klan meetings nowadays, as at drive-in movies, the primary attraction may not be what's going on up front.

The crowd may have numbered three thousand. It made a great standing half-circle facing the side of the flat-bed truck. A lanky, hollow-eyed young man in a dark business suit introduced the Klan chaplain.

"He is the pastor of a very famous church in Atlanta," said the young man, "and therefore he won't state his name."

The chaplain was in crimson robes with two vertical stripes of blue down the front. His head was covered with a high-peaked Klan hood. His eyes, seen through the slits, were shut. Spoiling the effect of mystery and majesty, there peeped beneath his robes a pair of white ankle socks and plebeian Hush Puppies.

The cross was lighted. Flames ate their way up the oil-soaked burlap in which it was wrapped, giving off billows of fat smoke. A Klansman on the truck, this one in white regalia, his face uncovered, played "The Old Rugged Cross" on a tape machine.

162

Calvin Craig, the Grand Dragon of Georgia, was introduced as a very talented young man. He had come, he said, to pay tribute to a man who was doing a great job—Governor George Wallace of Alabama. There was applause at that.

The chaplain, still hooded, returned with a Christian message which included this passage: "I challenge Martin Luther King to take his leaders and followers and go to Africa and teach his ignorant race so our churches won't have to take up collections and send people there to bring them away from the witch doctors."

And this: "Some of our great leaders are traitors to this country."

And this (a funny story): "Martin Luther King goes to heaven and is told that he can't get in without a white horse. Well, he goes back and gets the Kennedy brothers and he takes them up there. And Saint Peter looks at them and tells him, 'I told you a white horse, not a couple of jackasses.'"

The Grand Dragon of Tennessee, a young man who lost his left arm in Korea (a fact he alluded to for the purpose of saying that he was prepared to lose the other for what he believed in) admonished his hearers to stand in front of the mirror at home and to ask themselves: "What am I doing to fight communism?"

But it was Bobby Shelton's night. He hunched over the microphone, intense, thin-faced, unsmiling, and talked for nearly two hours.

It had been 97° during the afternoon and it was little cooler now. His audience steamed and dripped, but no drop of moisture marred the countenance of the Imperial Wizard. He admitted, however, to having some trouble with bugs. That was when he stumbled on the name of the White House press secretary, whom he called Pierre Sailinger.

"You've got to pardon me," said the Imperial Wizard. "Sometimes a bug gets in my mouth and sometimes it's just difficult to pronounce these alien names from Israel and Africa and other places."

It went without saying—not that Mr. Shelton didn't say it—that he was against "intregation," as he put it. But *he* saw the whole thing as a vast Communist plot which was using the Nigra, the soft underbelly of America, as a tool. (That conjured up a strange picture, the plotter chipping away at the foundation of democracy with a soft underbelly.) In any case, Mr. Shelton said, the Nigra was being "siphled up" and grasped by communism.

163

The Imperial Wizard was hard on the Press—not on those innocent victims of the publishers who laboured moistly in front of him,
but on the perfidious publishers themselves, who had performed a
"confistication" of the news media.

Mr. Shelton found it in his heart to say a good word for the late
Senator Joseph McCarthy, even though the Senator was a Catholic.
Time, said the Imperial Wizard, was bearing out Senator McCarthy's
"accusiations."

He warned his listeners to beware of the brainwashing "tastics"
that were used by the enemy, and suggested that they look into the
information that was being given their children at Bible school.

He told them he knew they were weary and tired of the long
intrusions of the weather, but he had more to say, and he said it—
about Communists, businessmen who have dollars on their eyeballs,
the Kennedys, Jack and Bobby Sox, the alien names of some of the
out-of-state students at the University of Alabama, and the rigged
pictures in the newspapers which purported to show violence being
done to Nigras in Birmingham, Alabama.

The fiery cross burned out long before Bobby, the Imperial Wizard, did.

You can't stand on no sidewalk down in Jackson, Mississippi

Jackson, Mississippi

As the fellow said about the Negroes of Birmingham, Alabama, a
few weeks ago, "Ah doan know what they complainin' about what
with Ol' Bull givin' them street baths and dawg shows evah day." Ol'
Bull is Birmingham's recently deposed Police Commissioner, otherwise known as Eugene Connor, a man whose rough exterior hides a
heart of stone.

No one would suggest that Jackson's mayor, Allen Thompson,
is another Ol' Bull. Mayor Thompson's exterior is silky smooth. But
he has something of the same solicitude for the Negro's wellbeing.
There have been no dawg shows in Jackson, or free baths. Rather the
police were out bringing in Negro youths from the cruel sun on
Capitol Street and sheltering them in the cool jail.

164

The temperature on Capitol Street at the time was 105° and the picking up of the Negro youths could only be interpreted as an act of pure kindliness, especially since they were not doing anything that looked faintly illegal. Some of them were carrying the Stars and Stripes, but, since this was Flag Day in the United States and the Stars and Stripes remains the national flag (even if only nominally in the South), it could hardly have been that that got them picked up.

Altogether, thirty-seven Negroes were taken off the hot streets and given rides out to the airy fairgrounds which have served as an overflow jail since the real town lockup became filled. Some nine hundred people have been lodged at the fairgrounds for longer or shorter stays in the past few weeks and Negro youths now speak of going to stay at the Fairgrounds' Hotel.

The police, in their kindly-gruff way, disavowed any humanitarian motivation and insisted that the youths had been arrested for parading without a permit. Since some of those transported had been walking alone, and some did not even have flags, this obviously was just a cover behind which the police hid their soft-heartedness. Even in Jackson, Mississippi, people do not get arrested for walking on the sidewalk. Standing on the sidewalk, maybe, but not walking.

While watching the Jackson police and men from the Hinds County sheriff's office performing their acts of Christian mercy, the attending reporters occasionally stopped to jot down or to exchange notes. For instance, it was worth noting that of the several police officers who escorted two youths to a police car—one of the youths was armed with a furled flag—one cop carried a carbine, and another had in hand a bat that looked as if it had been borrowed from Mickey Mantle. A reporter was jotting down a note about the way the cops were equipped to protect themselves from attacks with flags when a cop said, "Okay, get along, get moving." The reporter asked meekly what was the law about standing on the sidewalk.

"You can't stand on the sidewalk," said the cop. "There ain't nobody can stand on the sidewalk. That's the law. You can walk on it, but you can't stand on it. Git movin'."

A while later, a little old man stood leaning on a cane in front of Woolworth's. A cop stood at his elbow. The little old man was saying plaintively, "I will, but I just want to rest a minute first." The cop, humane to a fault, let him have his rest.

You *can't* stand on the sidewalk down in Jackson, Mississippi.

One man has been murdered in the struggle between the races. Heads have been cracked, bricks and bottles have been thrown. The trouble will become worse before it is over.

But in many respects, the situation is one of pure lunacy, of which the confrontation on Capitol Street was a prime example.

The Negro youths did not come to be on Capitol Street, with and without their furled flags, by idle chance. They had planned it. There had been a meeting in the morning at the Pearl Street African Methodist Episcopal Church where it was discussed what sort of demonstration could be tried now, all others, even a peaceful procession of ministers in twos down the street, having successfully got the participants a run out to the fairgrounds.

It had been decided, this being Flag Day, that some kids should go out and walk on Capitol Street, not in a parade, but singly or in pairs.

They began about 1:15 p.m. The police were already there, cruisers drawn up at various intersections, cops standing around them in blue (city police) and yellow (sheriff's office) riot helmets.

In Jackson, a parade is a parade is a parade, and no one need come forward with quibbling citations from Webster (a Northern integrationist anyway) that a parade must consist of more than a few people walking in ones and twos, far apart.

Now, *standing,* that's different. There ain't nobody can stand on the sidewalk. Not in Jackson, Mississippi.

So *some people save string and some people save snippets*

ITEMS COLLECTED BY A COLLECTOR OF ITEMS:

In Alexandria, Virginia, passersby saw a driver, who had smacked into the back of a parked car, stop, get out, and very properly write out a note and leave it under the windshield of the car he had hit. Police later disclosed what was on the note: "People who see me writing this note think I am leaving my name and address. But I am not."

166

The twenty-four-hour-a-day cold war (as reflected in a movie column): "The Russians will show in their country what they will call 'typical English films'—such untypical things as *Oliver Twist* and *Macbeth*. Wouldn't do to show British or Americans in a good light now, would it?"

Quote: "The right of choice was won when Cornwallis surrendered to General Washington at Yorktown, and I mean to defend that right. . . . Nothing has ever worried me as much as this. With our freedom challenged by communism on all the world fronts, the least we can do is fight to protect our rights at home."

And what was that all about? That was a red-blooded American father complaining about the school board which had ordered his son to get rid of a duck-tail haircut.

In a Washington court case, Witness A, male, denied knowing Witness B, female. Reminded that in a previous testimony he had said he had fallen asleep in bed with her, he replied: "You've got to know somebody for that?"

A man who had a hand in the preparation of President John F. Kennedy's speeches told the story of having been seated at a dinner next to Richard M. Nixon. When the talk turned to speeches, Mr. Nixon said there was one thing in particular in Mr. Kennedy's inauguration speech which he wished *he* had said.

"You mean," said the late President's aide, " 'Ask not what your country can do for you, but. . . .'?"

"No," said his table companion, "the part that goes, 'I do solemnly swear. . . .' "

A Dr. Jack D. Findley, who was in charge of an experiment at the University of Maryland in which a thirty-four-year-old man was isolated for 152 days in a small chamber, reported that the subject became a bit peevish before the experiment was over.

He became particularly peevish about his cigarette supply, which he got—in the beginning—by pushing a button twenty-five times for each cigarette. When the scientists put the required number of pushes per cigarette up to three hundred, the man inside nearly quit; when they put it up to five hundred he became "quite agitated."

"During the final stages of the experiment," said Dr. Findley,

167

"these complaints became even more intense, containing considerable aggression. In addition, suspicions and verbal aggressions directed toward the experiments and toward psychology in general emerged."

Verbal aggressions like: "Will you $%&#% quit playing with those @¢+*& buttons so that I can get my $%&*¢@ cigarettes?"

Life among the image-makers
(non-graven branch, obviously)

This capital, where memorials of all sorts abound, now has a suggestion from the President himself for the ultimate in memorials—a memorial to God.

He made the suggestion at the annual presidential prayer breakfast of a group called International Christian Leadership, which he invited to assume the task of raising the wherewithal.

The purpose of the memorial, at least according to the *Washington Post's* reporter who was there, would be to improve Washington's image as a prayerful capital of good and God-fearing people.

The President deplored the fact that statistics have advertised the per capita vices of Washington—in the bountiful society vices apparently are plural, like the two-car garage—but have not done full justice to its virtues.

The memorial to God—"a fitting memorial to the God that made us all," the President called it—would not be expected to dry up the capital's vices, but simply to create an impression of having done so. Its function therefore would be to serve as a sort of spiritual deodorant.

In the circumstances, the question may be raised whether the appropriate people to get up the memorial are churchmen, who in any event, may be presumed to have their hands full trying to improve the product without being called upon to worry about the package.

If it is image-making that is wanted, the place to turn is to the image-makers themselves. Under wise Madison Avenue direction, the fund-raising could be carried on with tag days, perhaps $100-a-plate dinners, which are very much the vogue here for fund-raising, and an advertising campaign built around the slogan: "Give, for God's sake."

168

It would beat the Red Feather.

In fact, the inventor of the $100-a-plate dinner, Matthew M. McCloskey, fund-raiser for the Democratic Party, recent Ambassador to Ireland, and favourite contractor to the Government, might make the ideal builder for the memorial. The Department of Justice has been making noises about suing McCloskey for undisclosed millions because of shoddy work on a Boston veterans' hospital. The firm has also been mentioned in the Bobby Baker affair in connection with the building of Washington's $20-million stadium. McCloskey is suffering, image-wise, as the saying goes, and might leap at the opportunity to find temporal improvement by throwing up a small temple. And, of course, if it didn't stay up, well, the Department of Justice could sue about that, too.

A solicitation list should not be hard to put together. Not long ago, Congressman James Byrnes (R., Wisconsin) bared all in a moist speech in the House of Representatives and said he had made a modest killing on the stock of Mortgage Guaranty Insurance Co., for whom he had done a parliamentary favour. He said he had done no wrong, but, inexplicably bent on atoning for it nevertheless, he volunteered to give his profits to charity. Perhaps if the money has not already been spent, it could be got back to be put to the good work of improving Washington's image. Mr. Byrnes at least would have the satisfaction of being able to say he *had* the next time a constituent said to him, "Do something, for God's sake."

Bobby Baker, himself, the former Secretary to the Senate majority, is another who might be called upon to help, even though the association of money-changers with temples has not been a happy one. Undoubtedly he'd be willing to help out in a project of this sort without demanding the hymn-book concession.

There are others, of course. If, in the beginning, an organ should be beyond the resources of the memorial committee, perhaps the place could make do for a while with a high hi-fi set and records.

Obviously the memorial should be built in the shape of the human heart, and of marble, a material of appropriately impenetrable hardness. Above the main entrance there should be the inscription, "God is Love," and under it, as a feature of the dedication ceremonies, a Mississippi congressman could shake hands with a Negro constituent.

The memorial would fly the United States flag as do other structures erected to national heroes.

169

Be *deciduous and merry*
fa la la la la la, la, la, la

Today, maybe right this minute, Lyndon Baines Johnson is down there at the LBJ ranch with Lady Bird Johnson and Lucy Baines Johnson and Lynda Bird Johnson and Little Beagle Johnson (that's a dog) and he's sitting down to a Christmas dinner that includes whipped sweet potatoes and toasted marshmallows. Ergh.

I got that about the LBJ's and the marshmallows on the sweet potatoes straight from the cookery column of the *Washington Post.* It will give you an idea of the sort of thing you are faced with in Washington.

Another thing for which I am indebted to that newspaper is that, for obscure reasons of its own, the *Post* had a reporter make a survey of the capital's strip joints, as a result of which it was able to bring us this happy Christmas note:

"A woman billed as The Cherokee Flash has a sequin ornament covering an appendix scar and she does a bump and grind routine to the tune of "Jingle Bells."

" 'She just started that this month,' a musician said. 'She said she wanted to do something Christmasy.' "

She could have put up a Christmas tree, goodness knows, but presumably a girl can't think of everything. However, it just happens that there has come down to us from a Druid forbear a little something just for Christmasy dancing girls.

In some places the following is sung (incorrectly) with the words "Deck the Halls with Boughs of Holly" (or Boston Charley):

> Deck your limbs with wreaths of holly, fa la la la la,
> la la, la, la,
> My, the green and red looks jolly, fa la la la la,
> la la, la, la;
>
> To each leaf a point attaches, fa la la la la,
> la la, la, la,
> If you grind, my, how it scratches, fa la la la la,
> la la, la, la.
>
> Doff each shiny leaf and berry, fa la la la la,
> la la, la, la,

170

Be deciduous and merry, fa la la la la,
    la la, la, la;
When the leaves have finished falling, fa la la la la,
    la la, la, la,
Run, the vice squad has come calling, fa la la la la,
    la la, la, la.

Needless to say, no one is allowed to be deciduous in a Washington nightclub.

So much for The Cherokee Flash and her undulant appendix scar. Long may she jingle.

A truly heart-warming Christmas story comes from Mamaroneck, N.Y., where little four-year-old Diane Petrillo has slapped a suit, and not a jolly red one, on old Claus.

It seems the child visited Santa's workshop at North Pole, N.Y., and got bitten by a reindeer. ("Down Dancer and Prancer, dammit; down Donner and Blitzen. You reindeer gotta quit biting the customers or you're going to wind up as dog food.") Anyway, little Diane's lawyer put in a claim for $6,000 damages, and, what with the Santa Claus business having fallen on evil days anyway, if he succeeds, there's liable to be a sudden surplus in the labour market, elf-wise.

According to the *Wall Street Journal,* which marks where every financial sparrow falls, an outfit called Santa's Village in Arcadia, California, went $74,000 in the red on a year's gross of $1.3 million. Santa's Village operates a chain of what it is pleased to call "tot parks." (Even before Donner, or Blitzen, or whatever one it was, put his fangs into Diane, the New York Santa emporium was already in trouble.)

But, to get back more particularly to the incident itself: there's a great chance here for something new in the Christmas novelty song line, an "All I Got for Christmas Was His Two Front Teeth," say, or "Rudolph the Red-Nosed, Buck-Toothed Carnivorous Reindeer."

Or something like:

There are venison chops (they're from Dancer),
It's Blitzen's left haunch that we'll roast,
There'll be stewing meat only from Prancer,
And soup bones from Donner at most;

171

Yes, I've bagged all of Santa's old reindeer,
But spare me from being reviled,
For I really do want to make plain dear,
I shot in defence of our child.

CHORUS:
I didn't mean to shoot them dead,
These creatures of the wi-yuld
Until old Dancer, he began
To ni-i-i-ble on our chee-i-uld.

I can see it on every jukebox in the country; it's got feeling.

Eyes glistening, we pass on, to what? Christmas shopping. Under how many trees this jolly morning were there His and Her airplanes from Neiman-Marcus, which is in Texas (where else?). They were selling for $176,000 the pair—$149,000 for his and $27,000 for hers. What's the world coming to? First it was twin beds and now Josephine's got her own flying machine.

But the present that would have caused old Scrooge to fling himself into the arms of the Ghost of Christmas Past and to thumb his nose at the Ghost of Christmas Yet to Come (if any) was the $400 survival kit. In it were caviar, pheasant, chocolate-covered ants (something to nibble on while waiting out the fire-storm), six bottles of Scotch (water substitute), six bottles of bourbon (Scotch substitute), and six bottles of champagne (for when the all-clear sounds).

Jingle bells, jingle bells,
Jingle loud alarm,
Oh, what fun it is to hide
Safe away from ha-a-rm.

(Repeat, gaily, and press on.)

Don't forget the gun,
Fight the neighbours back,
Drop them one by one
We won't share our snack;
Here we're safe from war,

Shelter's snug and tight,
Please to pass the caviar,
There's fallout out tonight.

And on that lugubrious note, a Merry Christmas to you, too.

172

Dear Mister President, Sir
I take pen in hand to write . . .

In his reply to a seven-year-old girl in Chicago who wrote to give him the benefit of her thoughts on a then-threatened railroad strike, President Lyndon B. Johnson said he hoped that all girls and boys would follow the news of their times and would always feel like writing him.

Dear Mister President, Sir:

I see where you told that Cathy May Baker out in Chicago that you'd like to hear from boys and girls who read their newspapers. Well, strictly speaking, I'm not one of your chillun, but I do read the newspapers, and I'm just a boy at heart. So I thought I'd drop you a line to let you know how I think you've been getting along.

Have you been in the White House much lately? All I ever see in the papers you are out in the garden talking to newspaper editors, or having a press conference from the Truman balcony, or shaking hands with tourists through the fence. All of this, I'm sure, is going to get you a good tan, but is it getting any work done?

I got a big kick out of the story the other day about how they may put floodlights on the White House to show it up now that you've turned out the house lights. Wouldn't it be cheaper just to turn the porch light back on again? If you still haven't convinced whoever it is you're trying to convince that you aren't a spendthrift, another six months of going around in the dark isn't going to do it. And you aren't going to be able to sleep nights with those floodlights shining in the windows.

That was a nice thing you did in offering to have all those Republican candidates in to get briefed on foreign affairs. I thought it was real cute—clever, I mean—how you said you didn't want foreign policy to develop into a partisan, knock-down, drag-out affair in the election. I bet.

I bet if you have your way those Republicans aren't going to be able to develop domestic affairs, space affairs, subterranean affairs or any other kind of affairs (including the Bobby Baker affair) into a knock-down, drag-out issue, either. They're already so hard up for something to talk about they're getting red in the face.

173

I see where Barry Goldwater said he wasn't going to come in for the foreign policy briefing. He probably didn't want to get confused with a lot of facts. Ha, ha.

I bet Richard Nixon felt good about your mentioning his trip to the Far East for the Pepsi-Cola Company, which his law firm represents, and how he may not have got much information on the political situation there since he was on a business trip. It may not have been much of a plug for Mr. Nixon, but it sure was good for Pepsi to get mentioned on the White House Lawn. Pepsi-Cola hits the spot—which is a good deal more than can be said for Mr. Nixon. Ha, ha.

I've been reading all about the new Cuba crisis that is supposed to happen and I'm a little confused. The Russians are going to get out, like you've been trying to get them out for two years, and that's good. But it means their anti-aircraft missiles will be turned over to the Cubans, which, I gather, is bad.

I see where some of the planes, though, are now equipped with new radar-jamming gear which will make the anti-aircraft missiles less reliable. That's good. But if the Cubans do manage to shoot one down, assuming they're going to try, that will be very, very bad. Then it will be necessary to bomb the anti-aircraft bases—or so some of the sterner newspapers and broadcasters have been saying some officials have been saying.

What I don't get is how you would explain to the world, not to mention the national conscience, how come you were bombing people for doing what you hadn't bombed the Russians for doing. I mean, that wasn't exactly a voluntary landing that Francis Gary Powers made at Sverdlovsk, was it?

I don't know, but it seems to me kind of chicken, having backed off from continuing reconnaissance flights over the Soviet Union (because it's strong), to say that you're going to go on flying them over Cuba (because it's weak). As for legality—well, it sure must make it hard for Dean Rusk to get out the words when he makes one of those pious declarations about the rule of law. It seems to me that if you fly over somebody else's territory you've got to take your chances, and if something gets shot down, well, tough luck.

I see by the papers, too, that George Ball, the Undersecretary, says that for allies to sell locomotives to Cuba would be very, very bad, much worse even than buses. I was glad to see he didn't say they might be used to transport troops for an invasion somewhere, which would have been even funnier than when it was said about the buses.

174

He put it strictly on the ground that locomotives would help the Cuban economy.

Mr. Ball said the United States was following a policy of economic denial. "Economic denial" is a five-dollar word for something which, if somebody else was doing it, would be called "economic aggression and export of revolution." Sometimes I wonder.

Yours wonderingly,

LITTLE GEORGE BAIN

All God's chillun got beagles, cowboy boots, chili an' kissin' cousins

Any parent can imagine the feelings that raged in our house when we discovered, thanks to *This Week* magazine, that with Lyndon Baines Johnson in the White House "toddlers are *Out* and teeners are *In*."

We had nothing around the house but this eleven-year-old, who was neither one thing nor the other. We thought for a while of sending him off to boarding school for a couple of years until he grew out of it, but eventually dismissed that as not coming to grips with the problem.

So eventually we traded him in on a power lawnmower, which we needed anyway. We were sorry to see him go, because he still had a lot of good miles on him, but that's the price you pay if you're going to stay in step.

"It's the miracle of the ages how LBJ has put his brand on the Capital of the Nation," said *This Week,* underplaying it. "It's LBJ's D.C. now. And proof of the pudding, pardon, we mean the deermeat sausage, is that all the natives of the capital ranch—a sort of newly acquired Washington extension of the Texas LBJ ranch—are living by the LBJ rules. . . ."

You see how it is. Any foreigner trying to get along necessarily takes his lead from such authorities as *This Week,* which takes its lead from the Royal Court, which takes it from the Monarch. In most practising monarchies, the ruler no longer exercises so great an influence on fashions and manners as in the 1700's but attitudes here have tended to remain frozen as they were before the break.

Thus, during the Kennedy administration, there was a sudden flowering of interest in high fashion and art galleries, and housewives who had been in the habit of going to the A & P for a can of peas took to going to the French market in Georgetown for a tin of *petits pois*. The essential difference between a can of peas and a tin of *pois* is twenty cents.

But to get back to *This Week,* the miracle of the ages, and what is now *In* in Washington and what is *Out:*

The reserved greeting is *Out* and affection in public is *In,* according to *This Week.* "It used to trouble people that the late President did not kiss his wife in public and eventually the Kennedys had to explain that they were raised in the Boston tradition of not showing affection in public."

Needless to say, anyone who was raised in the Toronto tradition would have to raise a mild disclaimer to any suggestion that he was among the people who were troubled by the President's not kissing his wife in public. According to Toronto tradition, a man will kiss his wife only behind closed (and preferably locked) doors, and then only if he cannot get around it.

In any case, public displays of affection are *In.* "Now," says *This Week,* "there is a happy feeling in Washington that around every corner you might find a kissin' cousin." There have been suggestions that things were pretty much that way around the Senate during Bobby Baker's heyday, but perhaps this is something different.

The City Slicker look is *Out* and cowboy boots are *In.* Terriers are *Out* and beagles are *In.* Chowder is *Out* and chili is *In.* Pink is *Out* and yellow is *In.* Cocktail parties are *Out* and work parties are *In.* (A work party is one at which Viet Nam displaces sex conversationally.)

"If the top rancher stops by (that's the President) he may have one Scotch. Moderation you know. And if the bash is held at the LBJ-WH ranch (that's the White House) the top rancher will check out early, say midnight, with a few ranch hands, to get a little paper work done before the morning round-up."

Galloping gophers, here I've been goin' around sayin' that a man "sashays out" when he leaves, and it turns out it ought to be that he checks out. But, I shore cotton to that "top rancher" talk, and other Texanisms like, "There's a man you can go to the well with." (The Republicans are saying he's a man the country can go to hell with, but they're a mean and ornery crowd, anyway.)

176

What else is *In*? Deermeat sausage, described as delicious for breakfast with hominy grits. The Texas recipe for it begins: "Take one deer and one hog and grind. . . ."

It's enough to give a man a twinge every time he looks at that power mower.

H*as Lyndon Baines Johnson turned anti-camuel-driver?*

Oh, undoubtedly there's something to be said for being President of the United States, but how many camel-drivers do you get to meet?

It says something for the Vice-Presidency—something like a rude word—that the one thing which got Lyndon Baines Johnson the most public notice when he was Vice-President was his bringing of Bashir Ahmad to the United States.

Bashir Ahmad was the friend Mr. Johnson made in Pakistan and invited to visit the United States if he could tear himself away from his cam-u-el.

Remember the "Legend of the First Cam-u-el" by Arthur Guiterman? It went like this:

Across the sands of Syria,
Or, possibly, Algeria,
Or some benighted neighbourhood of barrenness and drouth,
There came the prophet Sam-u-el
Upon the only cam-u-el,
A bumpy, grumpy quadruped of discontented mouth.

It remained for the then Vice-President to give the world the makings of the "Legend of Bashir Ahmad, the Celebrated Cam-u-el Driver," to wit:

"This somewhat pinched economy,"
Said Lyndon, full of bonhomie,
"Must make the going wretched for the workman of your sort,
So won't you park your cam-u-el
And visit Uncle Sam-u-el?
In Texas we've got wonders that are quite beyond report."

Said Bashir in perplexity,
"There is one slight complexity,

177

One doesn't leave a cam-u-el without a moment's thought,
I'm altogether sensible
He'd find me reprehensible
And grieving at my perfidy would die as like as not."

Said Lyndon somewhat haughtily,
"You're acting rather naughtily,
The invitation given was for you and not the beast;
Your friendly Uncle Sam-u-el
Plays host to no one's cam-u-el,
You come alone or not at all, it matters not the least."

Said Bashir then, "My attitude
Reflects no base ingratitude,
I'm really awfully thankful and astonished at my luck,
But in case the beast should languish
(To my everlasting anguish),
It would very much console me if I had a pickup truck."

So, no sooner had Bashir landed in the United States than he was whisked away to the LBJ acres in Texas, where there was a Ford pickup waiting for him, done up patriotically in Pakistan green.

No sooner did he get back home than good old Bashir blossomed in a small way of business as Karachi's friendly used-cam-u-el dealer.

And there, on the front of the lot, wearing on his twisty neck a sign which said, "Today's big special; owned by an old lady; never driven over forty-five m.p.h.," was: Guess Who.

Meanwhile, back at the White House cam-u-el drivers were as scarce as cam-u-els.

TRAVEL

The thing to do is don't

Down with the airplane
(except when I'm in it)

If anyone is of half a mind to get up a league of anti-travellers, I'd be willing to help out with a couple of slogans. How about: Getting There Is Half the Trouble. Or, Is Europe Really Worth It? Or, It May Be Fun Once You're There, but You've Got to Get There First.

(Once when BOAC was having teething problems with an aircraft that was widely known as the Lingering Giant, it was the fashion of competitors to bait BOAC people with a slogan: "Want to Arrive on Time? Go by BOAT." We don't want to single out particular carriers or modes of travel, but to present the case against travel in general. Still, that "Go by BOAT" reflects the sort of snide attitude that we should endeavour to cultivate.)

Perhaps I should make clear at the outset that my own anti-travel feelings do not reflect any prejudice against distant places, although, goodness knows, things happen in them that would never happen if one stayed home. Rather, they arise from a certain lack of affection, one might even say distrust, for the means of getting to them. This is particularly true of the airplane.

As an example of the sort of thing that may happen away from home, I would offer this: in 1958, the United States and British governments put troops into Lebanon and Jordan respectively. Air travel to the Middle East was disrupted. The day I wanted to go there was one flight, by the Dutch airline KLM, leaving London at eight in the morning.

It went to Amsterdam, thence, with stops of at least an hour at each, to Frankfurt, Budapest, Bucharest and, at midnight on a steaming hot night, to Athens. Dawn had broken over the Mediterranean before the plane lumbered into Beirut. Then, a change of aircraft, and on to Amman, in Jordan.

At Amman, British troops were installed at the airport and quietly going about housekeeping chores. The city itself was dead quiet, without a sign of trouble. If anything was going to happen, it

181

hadn't yet. It was the sort of calm which prompted that correspondent of long ago to write, "God sits on a little hill tonight overlooking this town. . ." to which his foreign editor replied, "Unmind war; interview God."

So there was nothing to do but to write a piece saying that all was quiet and calm and then—by now night again—to take it to the censor. After a weary hour, he took the copy and read it, blue pencil poised and lips moving in concentration. And when, after another weary hour, he had just got to the end of it, *blam,* someone set off a bomb that rattled every window in town.

That's a sort of shaggy correspondent story. But consider this: in no well-ordered community (i.e. if one stayed home) would a bomb ever, ever be set off so diabolically timed as to invalidate a patiently-carpentered account of the reigning quiet just on deadline. It fair takes the heart out of a man when it happens.

To give some idea of why I feel as I do about the *means* of getting from one place to another, I'd like to use an example from that same excursion.

An airplane taking off from the Jordanian airport at Jerusalem starts on level ground, proceeds briskly down a slope, clambers up the other side, and hurls itself hopefully into the air over the bald knoll that rises just off the end of the runway. I gather from the absence of news reports of spectacular crashes at Jerusalem airport that they usually make it.

The day I have in mind, the airplane, a poor spavined thing, well advanced into its aeronautical dotage, was loaded like a third class Mexican bus. The last three persons aboard were a CBS reporter-cameraman team with the ton of baggage that reporter-cameraman teams customarily carry, and myself. A clerk was overheard to say that "She is five hundred pounds over, but it will be all right." He was staying behind and could afford his insouciance.

The back of the aircraft was clogged with baggage. There were bundles in the aisles. The stewardess sat up with the pilot—although subsequent testimony in Washington about the ways of pilots and stewardesses would permit some doubt about whether this was a matter of accommodation or recreation.

The plane staggered over the knoll so close that you could see under the sheep.

In Beirut, staying at the same hotel, was the Middle East representative of the maker of that brand of aircraft. I told him about our overload. "Oh," he said, flatly. "You know, they regularly fly a

182

thousand pounds over our specifications, so if they had a five-hundred-pound overload on that flight, they were actually fifteen hundred pounds over."

With some vigorous chafing of the wrists he brought me around to the point where he could tell me about the day he found one of his client airlines machining a spare part out of an old piece of propeller stock to save the cost of buying the real article from the maker.

If there's one thing I can't stand in an airline, it's duplicity. And if there's another, it's making spare parts out of scrap. I'm an apprehensive air traveller. On any flight, I'm the little man scrounched down in the back seat, the seat belt done up tight around his middle, eleven sweaty fingers digging into the chair arms.

Once, in a fit of irresponsibility, the Canadian government gave me a course of training which included some instruction in the theory of flight. This had one effect on me (other than to keep me out of the army): it convinced me, beyond the possibility of persuasion otherwise, that launching a large glob of miscellaneous metal into the air and expecting it to stay there is a chancy business.

Consequently, little things put me off. One morning I turned up at London Airport when the fog was so thick that no prudent bird was venturing a step outside the nest. The man behind me was carrying a harp—a small, Irish-type harp, mind you, but an undeniable harp. That put me off.

Once, on a flight from New York, the aircraft taxied out to the end of the runway and then had to return to the ramp because a lavatory door had come off the hinges. That put me off. When the hinges on a lavatory door can fail, what about all those pieces in there whirling around and making those skirling sounds of metallic protest?

This is not to suggest that I have my doubts only about air travel. Far from it. The train is a prehistoric monster of green plush and soot which simply refuses to go quietly away and die in whatever swamp old trains are supposed to go away and die in. Ships are staffed exclusively by people dedicated to scoring one up on the passengers. Car travel is for people who make their own furniture in the basement.

Citizens, arise. Don't be lured into visiting the Exotic Orient. This isn't the year to see storied Britain. Europe can wait. What's so enchanting about Latin America that will compensate for the necessity of getting there to see it?

If those places want us as badly as they say they do, let them come to us.

183

The only good foreigner
is the foreign foreigner

For about two-and-a-half months every summer, Anglo-American relations (which would be fairly good if everyone but the Beatles and Danny Kaye stayed home) are subjected to the almost intolerable strain of mass personal contact.

In the business of analyzing the baleful influences that do evil to international relations, insufficient attention is given to tourism. A few thousand tourists complaining of not getting their laundry back can do more harm to goodwill in one summer than all the statesmen can put right in a year.

It is one of the great fallacies of the time that acquaintanceship breeds understanding; in fact, its direct and inescapable product is misunderstanding. Very many more people are murdered by their family and friends than ever are by strangers.

Contrary to the widely held belief that people need only to mingle to like one another, it is a discernible fact in Britain that the expression of anti-American sentiments increases in direct proportion to the number of Americans there are on hand.

Proceeding from this fact, one can say with assurance that the exchange of, say, half-a-million camera-slung tourists each year for three years would bring the United States and the Soviet Union to the point of war. The one sure-fire formula for peace (which henceforth may be cited as Bain's Law) is that everyone should stay home and should treat all foreigners as strange, far off people who are either impossible to understand, or not worth understanding, or both. It's matey-ness that's going to get us all in the end.

However, given long vacations and the ill-considered invention of the airplane, it is probably impossible to keep people apart. The most that anyone can hope to do in the circumstances is to ameliorate the effects of their coming together.

It is for that purpose, therefore, that the effort is being made here to correct some misconceptions of the sort that tend to give rise to bitterness.

For instance, should the North American visitor to Britain come upon Lord Plumport in cap, tweed jacket and rubber boots, overseeing the farrowing of a litter of pigs, it would be inadvisable to refer to him within his hearing as "quaint." Lord Plumport will have been a delegate to the last thirty-six Tory party conferences, and may even have taken his place in the Lords itself at times (to vote to maintain hanging, for instance). To describe him as quaint may be to invite a misunderstanding of the most painful sort.

There is a latent impression in Britain that all foreigners, and especially Americans, come expecting to find Ye Merrie Olde England, all yoicks-and-tally-ho, the streets awash with people in Beefeater costume, and falconry being practised in St. James's Park.

The natives are proud of their past, but quick to take offence at any suggestion that they are still living in it. They are wounded by the careless word which suggests the visitor thought to find them exclusively occupied in eating strawberries and clotted cream in rustic inns, or tending sheep and living in either ruined castles or in quaint cottages where the thatch hangs down like hair over a sheepdog's eyes.

It is difficult to know how such misconceptions arise. In any event, the visitor should be warned that it will do no good, once he has put his foot in it, to plead that his ideas were formed by reading those advertisements of the British Travel and Holidays Association which rely heavily on strawberries and clotted cream, sheep-tending, ruined castles and unbarbered cottages.

In opening a British fair in New York a few years ago, Prince Philip dealt with this question of misconceptions. Borrowing some of his propositions, what follows is an attempt to put the record straight. The "true and false" technique is used.

Proposition: ". . . Britain is not just an old country of tottering ruins inhabited by idle roués in eyeglasses, where yokels quaff ale by the tankard outside rickety pubs."

True. The incidence of eyeglass-wearing among idle roués in tottering ruins in Britain is no greater than anywhere else. Some of these idle roués have eyes on them like hawks.

Proposition: "Scotland is not entirely peopled by huge red-headed men in kilts and hairy legs who drink whisky when they are not playing the pipes and tossing the caber."

True. Fully half the people in Scotland are huge red-headed women in kilts and hairy legs.

Proposition: "There are certainly several harps in Wales and many fine singers, too, but the Eisteddfods are only a relaxation from work in the coal mines. . . ."

185

True. And when they are not playing their harps, singing in Eisteddfods, or working in the coal mines, the men of Wales, as any old movie-goer knows, spend their time plodding in black-faced lines, past the weeping women at the gates, carrying the broken body of young Gwyllym, who fell into the anthracite crusher. ("Look you what the owners have done now, Llewellyn; they've killed our young Gwyllym, the sweetest voice in all this black valley.")

Leaving Prince Philip's observations on the matter, probably not a moment too soon, one plunges on to consider some other popular misconceptions not related to the quaint and the picturesque.

Proposition: British telephones do not work.

False. This is a malicious story put about by a tourist whose arm turned to stone while he held the receiver waiting to put through an international call. In fact, the telephones work very well. It's the operators who don't.

Proposition: British cooking leaves a little something to be desired.

False. One needs only to ask any devotee of boiled cabbage, suet pudding and custard (alias yellow peril) to dispose of this canard. Finding this devotee of boiled cabbage, suet pudding and custard may take a little doing, however.

Proposition: A room for the night (as per British Travel and Holidays Association ads) can be had in any one of a thousand charming little out-of-the-way inns, with leaded glass windows, low beams, and gleaming copperware, for the equivalent of thirty-six cents a night (breakfast included, and a lunch packed on request for the next day's drive).

True. And I've been named Queen of the May.

O*n second thought, what say to a punt on the River Cam*

More and more people are going to Europe every year and more and more are hiring cars. As a public service, a few pointers on seeing Britain by car are offered here, arranged for convenience under several easy-to-read headings.

ROAD COURTESY: As very many writers of travel books have remarked, the courtesy of the British driver makes things easy for the visitor who, quite naturally, may find himself bewildered and ill-at-ease driving in unfamiliar surroundings, in a strange car, and on what to him is the wrong side of the road.

While still a pedestrian in London he will note the courtesy with which a driver will change down into first or second gear (depending on the power at his disposal) before driving over the tentative foot the visitor puts on a crosswalk at rush-hour. Changing down guards against stalling the car as it climbs over the arch of the foot, and thus ensures that the foot is subjected only fleetingly to the full weight of the car.

On the highways, the visitor will appreciate the way in which truck drivers, with a gay sweep of the arm, will signify their willingness to be passed as they approach the crest of a steep hill or the beginning of a blind bend. Sometimes the newcomer will make the ludicrous mistake of believing that the signal means that the road ahead is clear. Acting on this misapprehension, the visitor may be led into an exciting encounter which will provide him with material for a thousand stories with which to regale his friends: how much plasma was required, how they set the bones, where the stitches were put in, what the plastic surgeon said, and so on.

STARTING FROM LONDON: Even with maps, expert advice, and frequent stops to ask people on the sidewalk, the first-time visitor may find some difficulty in getting out of London. The usual problem is that he wants to go to Oxford but keeps winding up at Clapham Common or Ealing Broadway.

This problem is easily solved. Although it has been little publicized, it is a fact that can be vouched for from personal observation that 98 per cent of the traffic circles in metropolitan London have at least one sign pointing to *Slough And The West*. Some have as many as five of these, pointing in as many directions.

The simple solution, therefore, is not to start out from London at all, but to go to Slough—on foot, if need be—and start from there. Slough presumably is much smaller than London, which should help. However, not much can be said with certainty about Slough, since it is not known that anyone has ever got there and it may, in fact, merely be a product of some signpainter's whimsy.

SEEING THE COUNTRYSIDE: This is quite impossible. If that is what the visitor is going for, he might as well stay home. English cars generally are very low; English hedges generally are very high. The result is that anyone who is not passionately interested in the study of root diseases in yew hedges will not get a great deal out of the trip.

SUPERHIGHWAYS: This is one of those innovations, along with the telephone and household heating, which the Briton has long viewed with suspicion amounting almost to phobia. This has begun to break down, however, and a few years ago when the first forty miles of divided, limited access, high-speed motorway were opened, one of the metropolitan newspapers greeted the event with the simple heading: "Better than the Autobahn." This is known as British understatement.

Actually superhighways in Britain tend not to start anywhere in particular or end anywhere in particular. This leads the visitor to innumerable interesting discoveries, such as that he is lost.

HAND SIGNALS: Hand signals have not become quite extinct in Britain as they have in some parts of the world. Thus it is not safe to assume, when a driver is seen with his hand stuck out the window describing counter-clockwise circles, that his hand has gone to sleep and he is trying to restore circulation. He may be going to make a left turn. Or, for that matter, a right turn.

Knowledge of the proper hand signals is obligatory in the driving test which United Kingdom residents must pass and the visitor who wants to do the right thing will make at least the occasional effort. A backward patting motion means, "I am going to slow down." A forward shovelling motion means, "Go ahead and pass." A hand stuck straight out the window, finger extended, means, "Look, there's St. Paul's."

PECULIAR HAZARDS: Very many vehicles in Britain are diesel driven. The London buses are. So are most of the cabs. So are very many vans and lorries. After labouring the length of three blocks in the wake of a diesel truck in London traffic the lungs show up in an X-ray (if at all) with the appearance of the inside of a vacuum cleaner bag.

Getting behind a diesel truck on a long grade is to be avoided if at all possible. Sooner or later the driver will shift gears and as his

188

foot goes back on the accelerator, a black cloud of vapour will belch from the exhaust. If caught in this, there is nothing to do but stop until the oil clears off the windshield. The time may be passed in blowing smoke rings.

Now off you go. And the best of bloomin' luck.

When you've missed five hundred Kirmes the time to start is not now

The city of Soest has been celebrating its Allerheiligen Kirmes for nearly 550 years, which says something for the stamina of the people of Soest.

The Kirmes is an affair that is held every fall just after All Saints' Day. It is of religious origin and there are special services in the crowded churches on the Sunday.

But Sunday is only one of the five days of the fair, and on the others—*and* on Sunday afternoon and evening—the streets and hotels of Soest are filled with people singing their heads off, and stuffing themselves with *bratwurst* and whatnot.

Especially whatnot. This consists largely of drinking *steinheger* with beer chasers. Steinheger is a colourless liquid, a cousin to vodka, and the North Germans have discovered that it is efficacious in driving the damp from the bones, especially when followed by a glass of beer. Or so they say.

During Kirmes week there are steinheger stalls set up here and there in the streets to see fairgoers safely across the arid wastes between pubs, which are often fifteen or twenty yards apart.

For whatever help or warning it may be to other wayfarers bound in the direction of Soest in a chill November—and since Soest is the metropolis to the Canadian Army's NATO brigade, other innocents inevitably will be exposed—the following fragmented account is rendered.

10:00 a.m.   Still rosy with sleep, arrive Soest, guided by Canadian Army major, an old Kirmes hand. To Central Hotel where burgomeister and other Soest dignitaries about to open Kirmes by throwing out the first steinheger.

189

10:01   Given glass of steinheger, cup of coffee, bun a foot long with sausage baked inside. Former Stadtdirektor Becker makes speech, bangs table, drinks steinheger. Everyone bangs table, drinks steinheger. Gently press eyeballs back into sockets.

10:04   Waiter refills glass. Blanch.

10:10   Belgian Army officer recalls that similar opening of Kirmes last year span out all day. Left him strangely fragile day following. Sympathize with Belgian officer.

10:30   Party leaves hotel to tour town, via horse sales and machinery exhibits. Rendezvous for a small glass just inside east gate (built 1523-1526). Soest is one thousand years old, give or take a year.

11:00   Arrive new refuelling point. Man already poised with stone bottle ready to pour. Allow two glasses of elixir to be pressed on self and snap fingers at rain which has already soaked through raincoat. Sort of stuff that, given a couple of drops on his cheese, mouse goes out and licks daylight out of cat.

11:20   Little man in grey derby who says he's seventy-five years old, turns up and does head-stand on chair, meanwhile drinking glass of beer. Proves to have wristwatch on left ankle. Canadian Army brigadier, in front of whom feat performed, views whole unsettling performance with soldierly stoicism.

11:21   Retreat from range of man with steinheger bottle, who seemingly bent on destruction of guests. Saving self for play-offs.

11:45   English-speaking Soest native says come around other side of gate and view strangest feature of that historic relic. Turns out to be small room of all-too-evident purpose, jutting out from outside of building, with hole in floor. Soest native unnecessarily describes in graphic detail peculiar vulnerability of occupant to attack from below by arrow in time of strife.

11:46   Flee to rejoin rest of party.

11:50   March resumes in direction of Cathedral Square, where roller-coaster set up so that riders almost within touch of stained glass windows of ancient church. Streets filled with men in long, loose, green overcoats, green hats, and big clodhopper boots. Takeover by Jolly Green Giant and other pea-pickers?

11:51   Ask knowledgeable native guide how come this plethora of green-coated, green-hatted men. Farmers, he says. In *lodenmantel,* sort of farmers' uniform. Very clannish, farmers, he says.

12:20 p.m.   Party, not before time, arrives at Wild Man Hotel

190

where lunch to be given, obviously after few warm-up shots of steinheger. Wild Man Hotel (how about Wild Man Hilton?) filled downstairs with frolicking Soest people tucking into fat sausages, potatoes and what look to be boiled cucumbers. Possible to boil cucumbers?

12:30   When you've seen a thousand civic luncheons, you've seen 'em all. Decide to pass up this one. With equally soaked major, decide return to base. Stop for one steinheger on way, to discourage pneumonia. Snarl at stall-tender, just for sheer joy of it.

1:15   Light lunch.

2:00   Listen to suggestion from obviously deranged major to return to Soest in evening, when Kirmes in full fling, with much linking of arms, banging glasses and singing. Say, "Sure."

2:01   Wonder if not perhaps losing what few marbles remain.

Somewhere a hungry Hamburger somewhere a stuffed Canadian

My knowledge of German is negligible, or, as I sometimes say when the German-English dictionary is close at hand, *unwesentlich.*

Faced with doors marked *Herren* and *Damen,* I know which one to use without laying myself open to a particularly nasty sort of accusation. If I order a *Schweinekotelet* in a restaurant, I don't expect to get a lamb chop, and in the unlikely event that I order a bottle of Freundestueck Riesling Trockenbeerenauslese, I know what I am asking for, besides a breathtaking check.

I know *richt* from *links, Eingang* from *Ausgang;* I don't expect to catch a train at a *Flugplatz* or an airplane at a *Bahnhof;* and I know —now—that *essen,* in addition to being the name of an industrial city in the Ruhr, means "to eat."

All of which is merely a roundabout way of getting to The Lunch.

The ostensible purpose of my being in Hamburg was to talk with North German shipping people about their plans, if any, for putting more or bigger ships into the Great Lakes' service, to take advantage of the St. Lawrence Seaway. In truth, it was a convenient detour to make on the way back from Berlin, and I'd never been to Hamburg.

191

In any case, there we were, one reporter and one girl interpreter, in an office of the Hamburg municipal government. Could they put us in touch with some shipping people? But, yes. Phone calls were made and appointments arranged. But first, Herr Müller, one of the best informed men in town, an expert's expert on shipping, would stop by my hotel to give me the story in general. We might have lunch, it was suggested. And, yes, Herr Müller spoke English. Like a native.

So, back at the hotel, the guide-interpreter said she would go off and do some shopping, and meet me again in mid-afternoon. I told the porter that a gentleman would be coming in looking for me. Would the porter bring him to me in the lounge, where I would be doing some research in North German beer? He would.

And he did. In time he brought in a well-dressed, amiable-looking man of about thirty-five. We shook hands, mumbled names, and exchanged salutations, in English and German. I said, "Shall we have lunch?" and led the way to the restaurant door. He put his hand on my sleeve, shook his head, and steered out through the lobby.

Ah. Pal knew a better place to eat.

So we got in a Volkswagen. And then what seemed more likely was that this wasn't Herr Müller at all, but Herr Müller's emissary. A short drive and we would be at Herr Müller's office, or club, or house, or favourite restaurant; somewhere.

Pal drove through downtown Hamburg; through what may have been another municipality, all nightclubs, strip joints and saloons; through a substantial residential suburb. It had now become apparent to the alert reporter—thirty-five minutes of driving in silence gives a man a chance to think—that something was amiss.

"Whoa," I said. "Halt. On mit pullen der Brakenmechanischen."

Pal pulled over on to the grass; we were now out in the country. I asked him where we were going, and Pal told me—or maybe he was doing his celebrated funny recitations; I don't know.

I pointed down the road and made signs intended to convey the idea that I didn't know what was going on, which was no more than the truth.

"Essen," said Pal, in his frank, disarming way.

The last time I'd looked at a map, Essen was five hundred miles south, lurking under its smoke cloud in the Ruhr. Pal was obviously some sort of a nut, and a non-English-speaking nut to boot. Certainly no fit company for a homebody who had no thought in the world but to gather a few innocent facts about German shipping.

"Gebackmaken der Kraftwagen go," I said. "Back to Hamburg, Charlie, somebody around here has goofed."

Pal smiled, shook his head, poked one finger several times in the direction of his mouth—he's a crazy cannibal, maybe?—and drove on. Eventually, when there were still two or three miles left before we would leave Europe altogether, Pal pulled up at a restaurant. Nice place, with a view of a harbour—Stettin, Danzig, Kiel, Genoa, one of those places.

Obviously, out here there was no English-speaking waiter; out here they thought the Kaiser was still ruling. Pal and his guest sat down and resumed their scintillating banter, respectively in German and English.

"Ships," I said, nodding toward the harbour. "Big ships." (Hand signs here intended to indicate big ships. Pal looked doubtful and nodded to indicate he had got it: I had once caught a fish that long.) Pal was silent for a while and then said (I'm quoting from memory), "Graupelm felgerun mit der Erscheinung der Zeitung."

"By God," I said, "you hit the nail on the head that time."

Pal ordered lunch—partridge, I think; it still had some shot in it—and a bottle of wine.

"Good," I said.

"Gut," said Pal.

Excelsior. Communication at last.

Tapping myself on the chest, I said: "Kanadanische." Reporter? Journalist? News? I'm a little black sheep who's gone astray? "Zeitung," I said.

A light of comprehension lit in Pal's eyes—or it may only have been fever. Anyway, it was then his turn to play charades. He had a business card with a drawing of a microphone on it and jagged sparks radiating from it. Pal did dumb show of talking into his clenched fist.

Pal was a broadcaster. So what do you say to that? "Great. What do you hear from Walter Cronkite?"

Back into the Volkswagen, back to Hamburg, back to the hotel. Handshakes. Goodbye, Pal, whoever you are. Drop me a line. I'm in the book.

Somewhere, somewhere, there is a Herr Müller who was supposed to meet a Canadian correspondent for lunch one day in the lobby of the Europischer Hof in Hamburg, and another man who presumably spoke English, who was supposed to meet a Hamburg broadcaster in the same place.

If by some happy chance this should come to your notice chaps, I just want to say to the second of you—I hope Herr Müller bought you lunch. Yours was excellent.

Hannibal's crossing the Alps was like a day in the country

The movement of a family from one side of the Atlantic to the other is a relatively simple undertaking which, given proper planning and foresight, can be turned into something absolutely hideous.

Let us consider the case of a family which we shall call simply B—two adults, one male child, and a miniature dachshund—who were on orders to get them from London, by means of their own choosing, to report for duty in Washington not later than September 1st.

This instruction was accompanied by nearly six months' notice— and it is here that the First Lesson is to be drawn. It may be stated as immutable law that: The Complications of Any Given Move Will Increase in Geometrical Progression According to the Number of Weeks There Are for Making Arrangements. In short, if you're going, go tomorrow.

In the case of Family B, the head, as he likes to think of himself, sat down and, with that knack for cutting straight to the essentials that has made his name a byword wherever confusion reigns, decided that The Plan must be founded on two points: (1) his intention to buy an Alfa-Romeo at the factory in Milan, and (2) the necessity of taking holidays before the move, since there would be no opportunity after.

Condition (1) dictated the location of (2) and reservations accordingly were made at *Il Nido* (The Nest, bless us all) at a place called Fiascherinó, near Lerici, on the Gulf of La Spezia, which is also known as the Gulf of the Poets. Byron swam it and Shelley, unfortunately, did not.

194

Bookings also were made on a ship which would sail from Le Havre for New York on August 24th. Space was booked on a freighter which would leave the same port for Baltimore, with the car, the day before that. So far, so good—except for the dog. Obviously, the dog was not going to be transported by air to Italy to be brought back across France in a small car which promised to be loaded to the Plimsoll line, anyway, so separate arrangements had to be made.

In time, a veterinarian was uncovered who would keep the dog for a month, then transport it to Southampton. There the beast would be put aboard the same ship that would pick up the other, more human members of the family later the same day at Le Havre.

That took care of everything—except clothes. Since there would be different clothes needed for shipboard from those taken on vacation, a forwarding agent in London was instructed to pick up the trunks, hold them a month, then see them safely aboard ship, also at Southampton. With that, nothing remained but to get the airline tickets to Milan, make hotel reservations, and arrange to have money waiting to be picked up at a bank there.

Here we might pause to set down a Second Rule of moving: Any Money Arrangement Which Is Left to Someone Else to Make Can Be Counted Upon to Get Fouled Up.

But before exposing the working of this law in all its stark awfulness, it will be necessary to sketch in some background. The foreigner in Britain pays income tax on the money which he brings into the country. Got that? Consequently, if he is planning to be out of the country by, say, July 20th, he will want to calculate to the nearest penny how much he will need to live on until that date. But he will need to calculate, too, how much *additional* money he will need to bring in to pay the income tax on that amount of money. And, of course, when he brings in that additional to pay the income tax, he will need to calculate how much *further additional* money he will need to bring in to pay the income tax on the additional income tax money. And, when he brings *that* in—but, is it really necessary to go on?

In any case, it will be obvious that it would simply add another complication—not to mention that it would add to the expense—to bring money into England for the purpose of taking it straight out again for a holiday in Italy. So the subject of this case history wrote his Principals asking if they would simply send his pay in a lump

195

sum for five weeks in advance to a designated bank in Milan. And there was the family, all set up, with three days to wait before setting off.

That was the day the parents came home from a goodbye party and the motherly old dear who was playing keeper to the small child said: "I don't like the looks of young Christopher. He's coming down with something, if you ask me. Looks all glassy-eyed, he does, and he's coming out all over spots."

"Spots," cried the woman of the house.

"I don't know," said the keeper, "but I remember when mine had it and I think it's chicken-pox."

It turned out that as a diagnostician she deserved a write-up in *Lancet*.

Resolutely subduing the urge to lie down and kick his feet on the floor, the Head Man got the consent of the incoming tenants to an extension of time, cancelled two airline tickets to Milan—and flew off himself, protesting that he didn't want to go but had to if their reservations at The Nest were to be protected. What cash he had, he left with his spouse because (a) he wouldn't need it with money waiting in Milan, and (b) she would unless she was going to go on the dole. It is thoughtful little acts of self-sacrifice like that that endear him to all who know him.

In Milan he went directly to the appropriate bank, where an envelope awaited him. In it was a company cheque, with a nice picture of the company building on it and the correct amount in Canadian dollars neatly typed in. The banker said it was very interesting but that what it wasn't was negotiable. So the party under discussion telephoned Canada collect and cried a little and said that it was a fine, fine newspaper but Milanese bankers were extremely narrow about cashing dollar cheques made out by Canadian companies they'd never head of. And in no time at all—when he was not yet quite ready to eat his boots—the money turned up by cable.

And so, in due course, did his wife and child by air, the child no longer infectious but residually spotted and lightly dusted with face powder so as to avoid giving alarm to the Italian immigration agents. And after that, everything was fine.

Well, almost. It's true that most of the other denizens of *Il Nido* took to having one hinge at the spotty kid and moving off at a high rate of knots down the beach. And then, on the long, beautiful drive across France on the way to Le Havre, the new car took to over-

196

heating and once sent up a geyser which scalded the hand of a garage mechanic in Nice. And once along the way, for the first time ever, anywhere, they got bad food and were all violently ill. And by spectacularly bad management, they managed to arrive in Le Havre with two days to wait and hardly a franc with which to keep body and soul together.

And then, with money, clean clothes and a dog waiting for them aboard ship, the steamship company said that their papers weren't in order and, for an anxious hour, threatened to leave them at dockside.

All of which leads us to Rules Four and Five about travelling with a family:

Stay Single.

Stay Home.

Undefended the border may be but untended it surely ain't

According to the Moscow correspondent of *The New York Times,* *Pravda's* man in New York, Boris G. Strelnikov, has gone blubbering to his newspaper about some trouble the United States immigration authorities have been giving him about his visa.

Boris's main beef seems to be that the immigration people will not renew his visa without his being fingerprinted, a requirement which he and his colleagues find nasty and hateful. He also has some trifling complaints about being followed by men in grey raincoats and about people rummaging through his house when he is out.

It just so happens that there is a stoic not a thousand miles away who, until this moment, has not breathed a word about experiences with United States visas beside which Boris's are as nothing. Harassed Boris may be, but unusually harassed he cannot claim.

There's no use going into Boris's minor complaints. The experience of being followed by men in grey raincoats, or by sinister gnomes in black hats and running shoes, is one with which very many people have been familiar when walking the streets of a strange city on a wet night.

As for the other, Boris said he knew his apartment was searched

197

because he found his belongings out of place sometimes when he returned. This evidence seems to point only to occurrences of a well known natural phenomenon—that inanimate objects (car keys, for instance, and gloves) frequently change location when left unattended. They were put down right here, right on this very spot, and where do they turn up after a long and maddening search? Under this week-old stack of newspapers. So things are different in Moscva?

On the visa matter, the Soviet correspondent is on firmer ground, although he need not work himself into a persecution complex thinking the immigration people are trifling with him because he is a Communist. That's just their little way. For instance:

There was this time when the titular head of a small family which was being moved from London to Washington went to the United States Immigration Service on Oxford Street and asked what they would need to do to get into the United States.

They would need visas, he was told, and to get a visa he would need his passport and a letter from his employers saying why they were sending him to Washington, and for what probable length of time, and that he would be fully employed by them.

In due course a missive containing suitable assurances showed up, and the party in question called United States Immigration and said that he had the passports and letter, but, to save himself another possibly fruitless trip, could they say if there was anything else required. And the girl laughed and laughed and said wasn't it too bad that he had gone to all that trouble. The regulations had been changed. Canadians didn't need visas to enter the United States to stay, and vice versa.

"Are you sure," he said.

"Oh, quite sure," she said, "it's just been changed."

The scene shifts to Le Havre and the offices of a nameless steamship company. The S.S. *Nameless* is due to sail in three hours and a stained and travel-weary trio has just turned over tickets and other documents to be examined.

"Your visas," said the clerk. "You don't seem to have United States visas in your passports."

"No, you see, we don't need them. Not Canadians. Hands-across-the-border and all that. The regulations were changed just recently and Canadians don't need visas.

"Oh, no, no, no, no, NO. I couldn't let you get on that ship without visas. Why, do you know we could be fined $3,000—yes,

198

$3,000—if we landed you in New York without visas? Oh, no, no, no, no. . . ."

"But they said in London. . . ."

"Not according to our records."

"But, look, I have a letter here that says we're being moved there and for how long, and. . . ."

"Oh, that makes it worse; much, much worse. That says you are going to stay there and you can't. We could land you there only if you were in transit; if you were a bona fida transient; if you were just going to pass through on your way to Canada."

So they became transients, with six roomsful of furniture on another ship, marked for delivery to Washington, D.C.

The scene shifts once more to Toronto. The time is about three months later. A friendly and obliging officer of the United States consulate is saying:

"Well, of course, we'll give you a visa if you think it will be of any convenience to you. But you really don't need one, you know."

"I think I'd like a visa. You see there was that trouble in Le Havre, and having to give an undertaking to the steamship company not to stay in the United States, and. . . ."

"That was unfortunate. But really you can go back and forth with. . . ."

And that night at Malton Airport, he went to the United States Immigration desk and the immigration officer said:

"Where were you born?"

"Toronto."

"Where do you live?"

"Washington."

"Washington? You got a visa?"

"It's in the passport. At the back."

"Yes. Well, let's see. There's one form here we've got to type out and then we clip it right in with the visa, right in the passport, and then you won't get held up at the border again. OK?"

But he did.

Boris G. Strelnikov, you're a complainer. You and your lousy fingerprints.

This is the end

Johns Hopkins University's Laboratory of Applied Physics has produced what it calls a "mobile automaton": a robot which eats (electricity) when it gets hungry, plays when it feels good, sleeps when it gets tired and panics when it gets into trouble.

Panics when it gets into. . . ? By George, if it can type, we're obsolete.